ANCIENT CHINA

GREAT AGES OF MAN

A History of the World's Cultures

ANCIENT CHINA

by

EDWARD H. SCHAFER

and

The Editors of TIME-LIFE BOOKS

TIME-LIFE INTERNATIONAL (Nederland) N.V.

THE AUTHOR: Edward H. Schafer, Professor of Oriental Languages at the University of California, Berkeley, has taught Classical Chinese and Chinese Civilization since 1947. During World War II he served with the U.S. Navy in the South Pacific, and has travelled and studied widely, from Cambridge in England, to Kyoto in Japan. Professor Schafer is also a student of English history, ecology and conservation. Among his books are *The Empire of Min*, *Tu Wan's Catalogue of Cloudy Forest* and *The Golden Peaches of Samarkand*.

THE CONSULTING EDITOR: Leonard Krieger, University Professor at the University of Chicago, was formerly Professor of History at Yale. Dr. Krieger is the author of *The German Idea of Freedom* and *The Politics of Discretion* and co-author of *History*, written in collaboration with John Higham and Felix Gilbert.

THE COVER: Dressed in stately robes, an official of the T'ang Dynasty (A.D. 618–907) is represented in this figurine found in the tomb of a Chinese dignitary.

TIME/LIFE BOOKS

EDITOR
Maitland A. Edey

EXECUTIVE EDITOR
Jerry Korn

TEXT DIRECTOR *Martin Mann*
ART DIRECTOR *Sheldon Cotler*

CHIEF OF RESEARCH
Beatrice T. Dobie

GREAT AGES OF MAN

SERIES EDITOR *Russell Bourne*

EDITORIAL STAFF FOR *Ancient China:*
DEPUTY EDITOR *Carlotta Kerwin*
TEXT EDITORS *Ethel Strainchamps, William Longgood*
CHIEF RESEARCHER *Peggy Bushong*

The following individuals and departments of Time Inc. gave valuable aid in the preparation of this book: the Chief of the LIFE Picture Library, Doris O'Neil; the Chief of the Time Inc. Bureau of Editorial Reference, Peter Draz; the Chief of the TIME-LIFE News Service, Richard M. Clurman; Correspondents Erik Amfitheatrof and Takiko Kato (Tokyo), Lawrence Chang and Frederick Andrews (Taipei), Barbara Moir, Margot Hapgood and Katharine Sachs Pulay (London), Maria Vincenza, Aloisi (Paris), Elisabeth Kraemer (Bonn) and Mary Johnson (Stockholm). This international edition adapted by E. W. C. Wilkins.

CONTENTS

NOTE: THE PRESENT LOCATIONS OF ALL WORKS OF ART REPRODUCED IN THIS BOOK, AND THE NAMES OF THEIR CREATORS, ARE LISTED ON PAGE 187.

PREFACE

At the very beginning of our island history we were a small, peripheral part of a great Mediterranean empire. The Romans, who ruled the empire, knew that there lay, many months journey eastwards by caravan route across the mountains and deserts of Central Asia, a land where the Silk People lived; but they did not know that the Silk People inhabited an empire as large and civilized as their own.

Four centuries after its foundation this Chinese empire of the Silk People fell apart. Another century, and the whole northern half of China, including the metropolitan area—the very cradle and heart of Chinese civilization, was lost to the barbarian hordes. But whereas Rome fell never to rise again (for the Holy Roman Empire of the Franks revived the name only and not the reality), the Chinese empire was finally restored, and for three centuries, from A.D. 618 to A.D. 907, China was the richest, greatest, and most civilized power in the whole world.

Of course, "China" is not what the Chinese themselves called their country. The Silk People called themselves "men of Han", because their empire was founded by a Prince of Han; and the restored empire of the seventh century was called "T'ang" for a similar reason. Old habits die hard, for the Chinese to this day speak of "Han people" and "Han speech" when referring to the Chinese race and language, whilst in parts of South China which became fully acculturized later than the rest, "T'ang" is used in much the same way.

These two great peaks of development under the Han and T'ang dynasties fall within the compass of this book, which spans a period beginning with the magnificent, spirit-haunted culture of the Shang a millenium before the rise of empire, and ending with the refined, cosmopolitan civilization of Late T'ang and the beginnings of printing, that invention which, above all others, even gunpowder (another Chinese invention), brought the modern world to birth.

The treatment of this immense period is not, however, a chronological, school-book one of dynasties and dates. Instead, different aspects of its history and culture have been selected and described in a series of superbly illustrated essays, so that the reader may have the feeling that he is learning about the subject by means of a series of conducted tours, through the galleries of a large and sumptuous museum.

The magnificence of the illustrations are evident at a glance. But this book rises far above the level of the average run of picture books which proliferate so abundantly in this age of television and the "visual aid". What gives it its rare quality is, I think, the peculiar genius of Professor Schafer, a scholar who combines a passionate interest in the importance of *things* as a means of understanding the past, with a profound insight into the religious, intellectual and ideological processes by which the past was moulded. To my mind China in the period of her ancient greatness comes extraordinarily alive under this treatment.

DAVID HAWKES
Professor of Chinese
Oxford University

ARAL SEA
Lake Balkhash
ALTAI MTS.
R. Jaxartes
FERGHANA
KUCHA
Slave market
TIEN SHAN
TARIM BASIN
TUN-HUANG
Buddhist caves
R. Oxus
SOGDIANA
KHOTAN
Jade centre
PAMIRS
K'UN LUN MTS.
HINDU KUSH
RED BASIN O
TIBET
R. Indus
HIMALAYAS
WEST
KAPILAVASTU
Buddha's birth place
R. Ganges
INDIA
BURMA
印度國

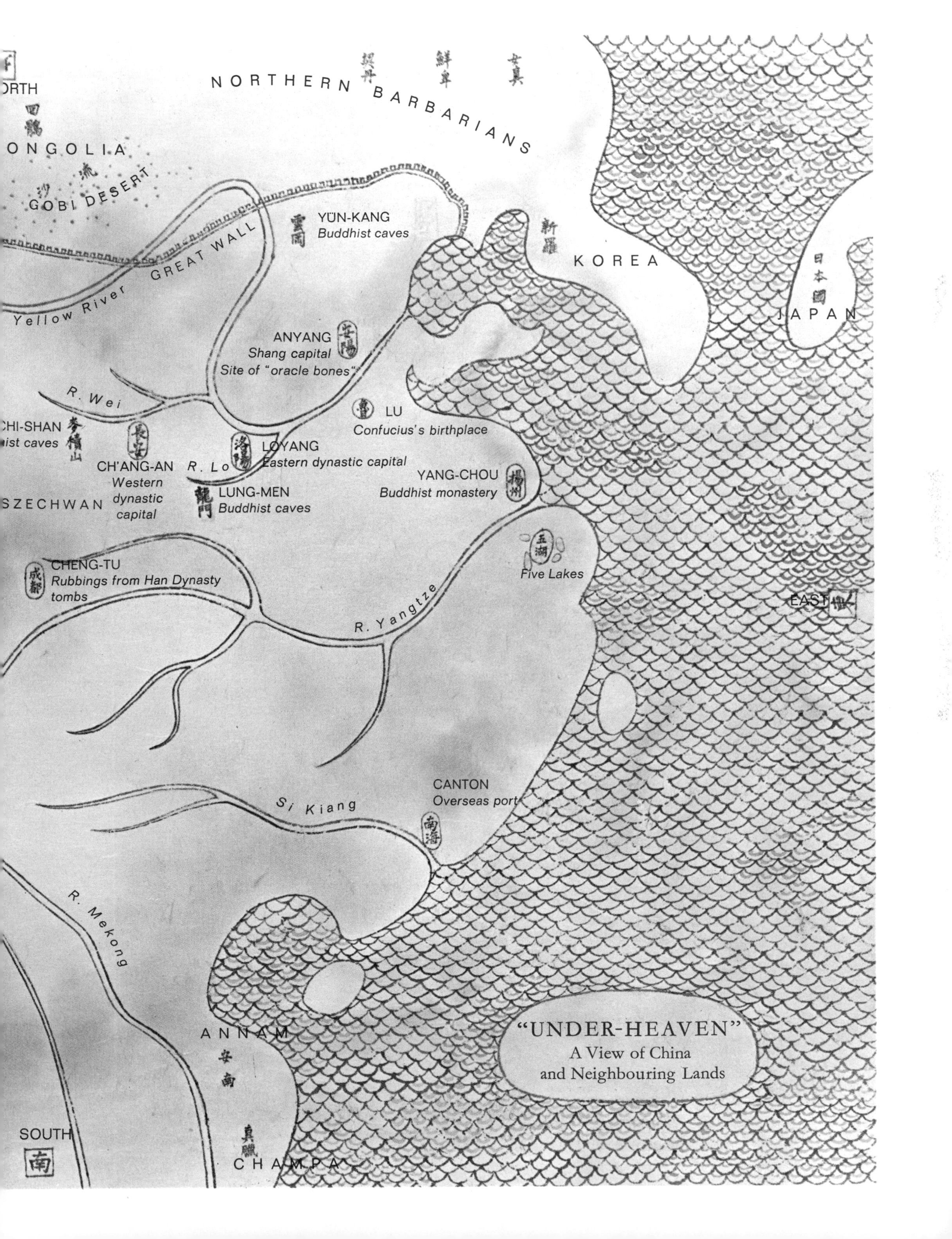

"UNDER-HEAVEN"
A View of China
and Neighbouring Lands

1

THE MIDDLE KINGDOM

THE SOVEREIGN FU HSI, *a legendary figure of the third millennium* B.C., *is revered as one of China's first wise men. He is depicted here as the inventor of the eight symbols used in divination (lower left), which he is said to have discovered by studying the markings on the shell of a tortoise (right).*

In 481 B.C. the lord Szu-ma Niu was driven by rival barons from his fief, one of the many walled towns of nothern China, and he set forth on a long journey to the south in search of a new land-holding. His destination was the State known as Wu near the mouth of the great Yangtze—a region he considered hardly civilized.

Szu-ma Niu differed from the other numerous feudal barons of his age only in the later distinction of one of his teachers—a sage now known as Confucius. Through Szu-ma Niu's eyes we may glimpse the China of 2,500 years ago, as it appeared to an upper-class observer of the time.

To him the centre of the world was a cluster of little city-States in the flood plain of the Yellow river and its adjoining foot-hills. He did not call this homeland "China"; that alien name was still to be invented. If someone had asked Szu-ma Niu who he was—to identify his proud but troubled people in the Central Plain—he would probably have asserted with confidence that he and his fellows were the Hua people and would have spoken of his homeland as central Hua to show his sense of ethnic and cultural identity. In another situation he might have emphasized his geographic location by calling himself a man of the Middle Kingdom—according to Hua belief, the centre of the habitable world; or if politics and recent history had been on his mind he would have proclaimed himself a man of the Chou Dynasty. But most likely he would have preferred to give his local identity, calling himself a native of Sung, his little city-State.

Szu-ma Niu's homeland was not very different from the northern China of today. If he had halted his chariot on a hill-side for a last look at it, he would have seen a dry, dusty plain that extended far beyond the horizon to the north, and through it weaving a wide, sluggish river, heavy with yellow silt from distant mountains. The yellow dust had blown out of Mongolia for thousands of years to cover the land to a depth of many yards. Subject to constant erosion by the winds, and by the little remnant of rain brought up from the South China Sea in the summer season, the farmlands were frequently flooded by the great river when it choked with silt. These were the two great facts of Szu-ma Niu's world: the dust and the river. He thought of them as "Yellow Earth" and "Yellow River".

Surveying his homeland, Szu-ma Niu would have seen a few residual patches of forest on the plain. The depletion of the ancient oak woodlands for material for houses, furniture and fires had been great. But there was still enough forest cover in the watershed of the Yellow river to provide food and shelter for many native animals. There were deer in plenty for the arrows of the hunter, and the familiar songs of Szu-ma Niu's childhood made much of the beautifully coloured wild ducks on the river margins and the bush warblers that sang sweetly among the lilacs and spireas. The dwindling forest also protected larger and more fearful animals. Elephants and rhinoceroses could still be found occasionally in the highlands of the southern frontier. They too were part of the world of Szu-ma Niu. Venerable books told him that the huge beasts had once overrun the land, along with other unimaginable monsters, until they were driven away by the good and valiant kings of old.

Everywhere in the lowlands Szu-ma Niu would have observed fields of millet and barley, traversed by slow ox-carts on dusty roads and spotted with houses of mud, wood and thatch. At intervals stood strongholds of the kind he himself had governed, surrounded by massive earthen walls.

The civilization that Szu-ma Niu took for granted in the fifth century B.C. had deep roots in the Stone Age, over a thousand years before. His remote unknown ancestors, the first farmers of China, had valued jade, just as he did, and had used tripod cauldrons of earthenware designed exactly like the bronze ones he often saw on the altars of the gods. But Szu-ma Niu had only the haziest notions of that prehistoric era and its primitive culture. He was better informed about those who had ruled the Yellow river plain from 1500 to 1000 B.C., more than 500 years before his time.

They were the kings of Shang, rulers of a primordial agricultural nation with a rich religious and ceremonial life. Today they are famous for the handsomely designed ritual vessels, skilfully cast in bronze and engraved with sacred symbolic figures, that were used in elaborate dramas honouring royal ancestors and fertility gods. Szu-ma Niu's vision of that remote age—of chariot-borne bowmen, great royal hunts, wise astrologers and monarchs seated in pillared halls—was undoubtedly coloured by fanciful traditions. To him, the early kings of Shang, whose names he had memorized as a child, were men of divine virtue, worthy of almost religious veneration. Theirs had been an era comparable in spirit to the heroic age celebrated by Homer in the West.

About 1000 B.C. the Shang nation had been overrun by the warlike Chou people from the west. The new masters of the Middle Kingdom were quickly assimilated into the old agricultural theocracy of Shang; the royal hunts continued, bronze-clad knights still rode their chariots and human victims were still sacrificed at royal graves. In time, however, the authority of the Chou kings declined—perhaps as a result of their custom of granting huge fiefs to royal sons and brothers—and an age of feudal separatism set in. By the fifth century B.C. the Chou ruler was little more than a figure-head, clothed in rich ceremonial robes, performing archaic rituals in his holy city of Loyang, quite divested of political power. The realm was divided among petty city-States that came and went like the seasons. Szu-ma Niu himself had been involved in an unsuccessful insurrection, and his present journey was the result.

The very name Szu-ma Niu is symbolic of the age of unrest and change in which its bearer lived; this was a period not only of political but also of technological revolution. His surname Szu-ma meant "Master of the Horse", indicating a dignity that had become virtually hereditary in the baro-

A RITUAL VESSEL, *this three-legged cauldron is decorated with a monster mask often found on bronzes of the Shang period. The mask's highly stylized design—silhouetted here against a grey-green background—includes two dragons facing each other in profile.*

nial family to which he belonged. His given name, Niu, meant "Ox". He also had other names, as was the custom in those times among men of good breeding. These extra names were usually suggested by the original given name. The fact that Szu-ma Niu's added names were Keng ("Tillage") and Li ("Plough") reveals a significant development: the age of the ox-drawn plough had arrived.

Coupled with the substitution of animal traction for human labour came another remarkable new invention—cast iron. While the knights and barons who ruled the land continued to wear the bronze helmets of another age and to wield bronze swords in battle, ordinary farmers were coming more and more to depend on iron tools to perform the daily labour that produced food for the kingdom. But although more crops were being grown and more people were digging and planting in the Chinese loam, times did not seem to be getting better. In this age of aristocratic bronze and peasant iron, old institutions were decaying, old allegiances were dissolving and few men felt confident that the accepted order of things would be tomorrow as it was today.

This atmosphere of personal anxiety and political conflict, of moral disturbance and intellectual ferment, was to produce an era that would be known as China's classical age, when her greatest heroes and wisest philosophers walked the earth. One of the latter was a man named K'ung Ch'iu. Szu-ma Niu was a disciple of K'ung Ch'iu, and many of his contemporaries admired the teacher as one of the wisest of those who travelled from one baronial hall to the other, offering advice on correct behaviour and enlightened political practice; they probably did not regard him as more than that. But K'ung Ch'iu's reputation as a sage was to be greatly enhanced after his death and he was ultimately to be venerated as a god. We know him as Confucius.

Doubtless Szu-ma Niu endured some agony of spirit as he left his friends in the north to take up his life among the unknown strangers of the southeast. To him, as a Hua man, the Middle Kingdom was a beacon of civilization to the benighted heathen who inhabited the shadowy realms of both the north and the south. The peoples of the far north —the herders of sheep, horses and camels on the grassy steppes, as well as the hunters of gazelle and elk on the forest margin—were to become the ancestors of the Turks, Manchus and Mongols who later would be feared as raiders and looters. But in those days the northern frontier was fairly stable, and defensive walls, built by the northernmost city-States, usually kept the mounted warriors out of the good lands of millet and wine. Eventually these walls would be joined together to make the Great Wall of China, but the unified central government needed for that immense task of engineering did not exist in Szu-ma Niu's day.

To men of Szu-ma Niu's class, the menacing nomads were hardly human. They called the most dangerous of them "dog people", classifying them among the wild beasts. They also applied that label to their non-Chinese southern neighbours—the Man people (also called Miao, Mao, Min and Mang) who probably spoke tongues related to Thai, or to Burmese and Tibetan.

The "dog" epithet was believed to derive from an ancient myth that was known to the Hua people and that was later accepted by the southern "Dog Men" themselves. The old tale told that all the Man people were descended from a wonderful dog, P'an-hu. Long ago, according to the tale, a king offered his daughter in marriage to the hero who would bring him the head of his enemy, a mighty warrior. One of his own dogs carried out the dangerous mission successfully and the reluctant monarch was obliged to yield his daughter to the triumphant dog, which carried her off to a new home in a cave in the far south. There, the legend says, she bore him a dozen sons and daughters and from these half-human hybrids sprang all the non-Chinese races of the South. In medieval times, centuries after Szu-ma Niu's lifetime, some of the southern aborigines continued to offer sacrifices to their great canine ancestor. He is still remembered by the modern Miao peoples, and is especially revered by the Man tribes of northern Vietnam.

The haughty minds of the early Hua men also envisaged the savage rice cultivators of the subtropical valleys as reptilian, slithering nastily on the dark southern frontier. A book already old in Szu-ma Niu's time characterized the inhabitants of the central Yangtze basin:

How they writhed, the Man in Ching,
Playing the rival to our great domain!

The ancient attitude was reflected in other ways. In Hua writing, many of the characters representing the names of these outlanders incorporated the figure of a reptile; still other graphs depicted them as apelike. By the fifth century B.C., ancient practices, such as head-hunting and human sacrifice, were becoming less respectable among the Hua people and it was convenient to attribute them exclusively to the Man people—mere submen, caricatures of the Hua Chinese.

Looking ahead to his new southern home, Szu-ma Niu may well have shuddered. But distasteful as was the prospect of a career among men whose veneer of culture was still very thin, the track he took was to be followed by many generations of Chinese, who would gradually come to accept the Wu region as part of their territorial heritage.

It was a richly diversified landscape into which Szu-ma Niu rode, very different from the monotonous yellow plains of the old country. Tiny hornless deer fled shyly through streamside bamboo groves, and sweet-singing bulbuls fluttered among the white magnolias and purple paulownias. The traveller could imagine the almost legendary alligators that bellowed in the tepid lakes ahead of him. If he went all the way to the great Yangtze he might even rejoice in the antics of black porpoises and river dolphins. Strangely and fearfully attractive to him, this youthful land would become a realm of romance for his descendants, the home of rainbow goddesses, ecstatic priestesses and lotus-gathering girls. Still later, it would become the great mother of gardens, nourishing the arts of poetry and painting alike.

The 200 years following the journey of Szu-ma Niu were bitter years for his homeland. The struggle among the city-States became intensified between the fifth and the third centuries B.C. and the smaller ones were swallowed up by the larger.

But the Chinese world was expanding out of the Yellow river basin towards the south—conquering, absorbing or eliminating—in any case, ultimately dominating the peoples it encountered. It was inevitable that these barbarians should become Hua men. There was little visible physical difference between them and the new arrivals. To become a Chinese, it was only necessary that a Man tribesman learn to speak the Chinese language, write the Chinese script and accept the rule of the Chinese King, along with the social and moral doctrines that prevailed in the Middle Kingdom. The only handicap would be that some northerners might still regard him as a second-class Chinese; true respectability required birth in the Middle Kingdom itself.

The Hua men had to acknowledge that the new, savage lands they were appropriating provided many useful things. From the natives of the rich south they obtained stones and metals, handsome pearls and feathers for the ceremonies of their Courts and temples, and bamboo and rhinoceros hides for the arrows and breastplates of their aristocratic fighting men. The despised Man people even knew arts and skills that might profit the

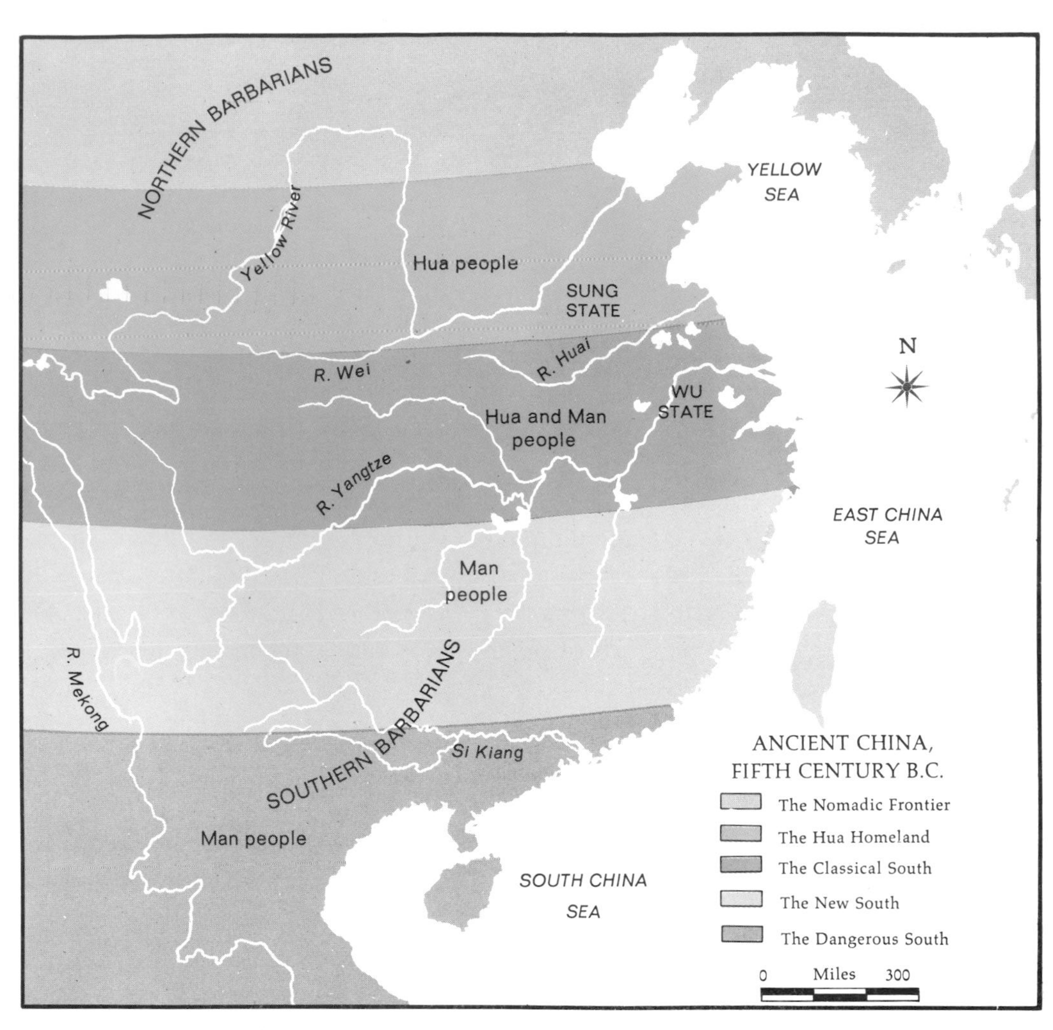

THE PEOPLES OF EARLY CHINA *lived in five broad areas. The Hua people inhabited the north central region, on the Yellow river plain. North of them lived fierce nomads, with whom the Hua were constantly warring. The Hua settled in the Yangtze basin in the Classical Age (600 B.C. to A.D. 200), living among the Man people, whom they introduced to civilization. After the fall of the Han empire, many Hua went into the "New South" and "Dangerous South", in spite of their fear of the "barbarous" Man natives.*

proper masters of the world. The Middle Kingdom was rich in such basic goods as cereals, salt, silk and hemp textiles and all sorts of lacquered utensils and furniture. Still, in the past it had also imported things from the strange men on all its frontiers. The inhabitants of the great northern forests, beyond the control of the King, had sent gem-stones and deer bones and sinews for bows. It was not difficult for the Hua men to admit that the best arms and armour, or the materials for them, had to be obtained from unlettered aliens. But it was less easy for them to acknowledge, or even to realize, that they borrowed *ideas* from foreigners. Yet in fact they did.

Much of the spiritual and imaginative part of Chinese civilization—much of what we now think of as typically Chinese—originated among the proto-Thai peoples of the south, the proto-Tibetan peoples of the west and the proto-Mongolian peoples of the north. The huge burial mounds of the early Chinese emperors apparently had their origin in the plains of Central Asia; the popular tales about fox-fairies that permeate Chinese literature probably began among the forest-dwelling hunters of Manchuria; the arts of cultivating rice and domesticating cattle were doubtless adopted from the despised races of the remote south; the Chinese reed organ came from the tropical jungles; the Chinese cult of Heaven shows affinities with one in the northern steppes.

Chinese culture, both material and spiritual, grew rich because the plains of the Yellow river valley became a cross-roads used by many peoples, a centre of commerce and political negotiations and hence a focus of every kind of custom and point of view.

In the middle of the third century B.C., political order was restored in the Middle Kingdom by the western city-State of Ch'in, whose rulers gradually extended their control over the eastern plains.

The Ch'in empire proved to be short-lived; after the death of its first ruler Shih Huang Ti, it dissolved into another contest among ambitious barons. But before the end of the third century, the old Middle Kingdom and the warm Yangtze watershed were again united under the aegis of the famous empire of Han, the peer of Rome and the master of the Far East for the next four centuries.

The Han Dynasty emerged in 206 B.C. under the leadership of a commoner, Liu Pang, a military officer who rose from the ranks to seize power in the vacuum created by the collapse of the Ch'in empire. As in the case of Han's Western counterpart, the Roman Empire, successive leaders extended Han's boundaries by military conquest. Their armies marched far into the endless haunted forests of the hot south below the Tropic of Cancer, and they established permanent colonies in Korea and Central Asia. Caravan routes leading westwards to Persia and Rome were opened up, inaugurating a great period of international trade based on the universal demand for Chinese silk.

Heady and exhilarating though it was, the Han imperial power lacked theoretical and moral justification. That was supplied by the creation of an edition of ancient documents that solidified into dogma certain useful opinions of the wandering teachers of the Chou era, particularly the teachings of Confucius. These fragmentary "classics" became in Han times orthodox canon, the basis of accepted opinion on manners, morals and government. Writings of the old rival schools of thought that seemed not to represent the true views of Confucius and his followers were either censored or destroyed. Han scholars and scribes then set to work putting the acceptable books into a shape that conformed to the taste of their era; many were full of textual errors, relics of barbarism and almost forgotten mythology. A partly imaginary past was created out of the heritage from the Chou period, and the customs and traditions of the old world of barons and knights were thus adapted to a new society. From the respect for learning that resulted was to come, over the course of centuries, the identification of the scholar with the gentleman; from it was to come, also, the power of the huge scribal bureaucracy that dominated Chinese life and thought through the medieval era and into modern times. Scholarship became the tool of empire.

However, the newly compiled "Confucian Classics" and their Han editors did not escape criticism. Probably their severest critic was a man named Wang Ch'ung, a scholar of the first century A.D. Wang Ch'ung led a lonely life; he was too clever and critical for his own good. Born in a coastal town in the south country—a social disadvantage in itself—he took the northward road from the Yangtze valley to the late Han capital of Loyang in the old Middle Kingdom. He was an orphan, but he must have gone to Loyang under high auspices; he studied under Pan Ku, one of the best historians of the age. He was so poor that he could not afford to buy books, but had to read them where they were displayed for sale in the city's shops. Fortunately he had a tenacious memory and soon became familiar with all doctrines and opinions, both past and present (or so he believed). When he returned to his home province he became a teacher of promising youths, after an attempt to hold an official post failed because his sharp mind and caustic tongue alienated others. But he understood his age as few men did and summed it up in a remarkable book, the *Lun Heng* ("Arguments Weighed").

The *Lun Heng* is today probably the single richest source of our knowledge of Chinese intellectual and religious life in the first century A.D. But in Wang Ch'ung's time his work never became widely popular because he freely attacked fondly held beliefs, not even excepting the honoured views of the Confucian scholars. All idols, both popular and academic, were his targets. He sought truth through experience, guided by reason, rejecting both ancient authority and the common testimony of mankind as guides to certainty. The sacred texts of the past, he thought, were seriously corrupted; the golden age they claimed to describe was mythical. He speaks about the difference between the true Hua men of Han times and the hordes of barbarians that surrounded them:

> *That which makes the several kinds of Hua men nobler than pagans and savages is their comprehension of documents about humane and responsible conduct and their understanding of the scholarship of ancient and modern times.*

A century after the death of Wang Ch'ung the first era of Chinese domination over the peoples of the East ended. In A.D. 220 the glory of Han collapsed in the contest for power between Court factions and great landed families, in popular religious and revolutionary movements, and finally in a struggle among great provincial warlords. The classical world in whose beginnings Szu-ma Niu had taken part, and whose final years had been scrutinized by the poor provincial teacher Wang Ch'ung, was giving way to a new age.

During the next 400 years, between the third and the seventh centuries A.D., many ephemeral nations rose and fell on the sacred soil of China. The old Middle Kingdom shuddered as barbarian hordes from the north dashed through the streets of the old cities, riding their hardy ponies and waving their curved bows. For long periods, segments of the Yellow river valley were ruled by petty chieftains of diverse origins—some Tibetan, some Mongolian, some Manchurian. The proud Hua people were compelled to accept the hateful role of a subject race, serving illiterate aliens who stank of butter, koumiss and other unthinkable substances.

Unwilling to serve such unpleasant masters, many members of the old northern aristocracy who survived the invasions fled southwards. They retraced the long-vanished footprints of Szu-ma Niu into the pleasant land of Wu at the mouth of the Yangtze, and even farther south where short-lived dynasties ruled over a mixed Man-Hua population. Among the emigrant Chinese *literati,* especially the younger ones, the disasters that had shattered an ancient way of life produced disillusionment with established beliefs (Wang Ch'ung would have been gratified), hope for a new faith—and universal bewilderment. Some of them became vagabonds, eccentrics or voluptuaries. Others became recluses, visionaries or subtle dialecticians. Altogether, they were a generation in ferment. But nervous and uncertain as it was, this new generation was producing a new China.

The very nature of their environment had much to do with this. The practical men among the emigrants were excited by the discovery of new herbs and trees, new mines and quarries. Followed by pioneer farmers, they began to strip the subtropical hill-sides. Firewood was needed, and timber for buildings. The expanding bureaucracy needed unlimited supplies of carbon-black ink, taken from pine wood. Aromatic and medicinal barks were found in great abundance. Mercury and gold lay in wait under the soil, in amounts that must have dazzled the former inhabitants of the bare Yellow river valley. The rich wilderness was endless, and no one thought about its conservation.

Literate, sensitive men, whether urban sophisticates or forest hermits, were learning to take delight in their new surroundings. The feeling for nature—and the rich poetry and painting that ultimately sprang from it to become the glory of Chinese culture and attract the homage of the world—were nurtured in this era of expulsion, defeat and alienation.

A DYNASTIC CHART OF ANCIENT CHINA

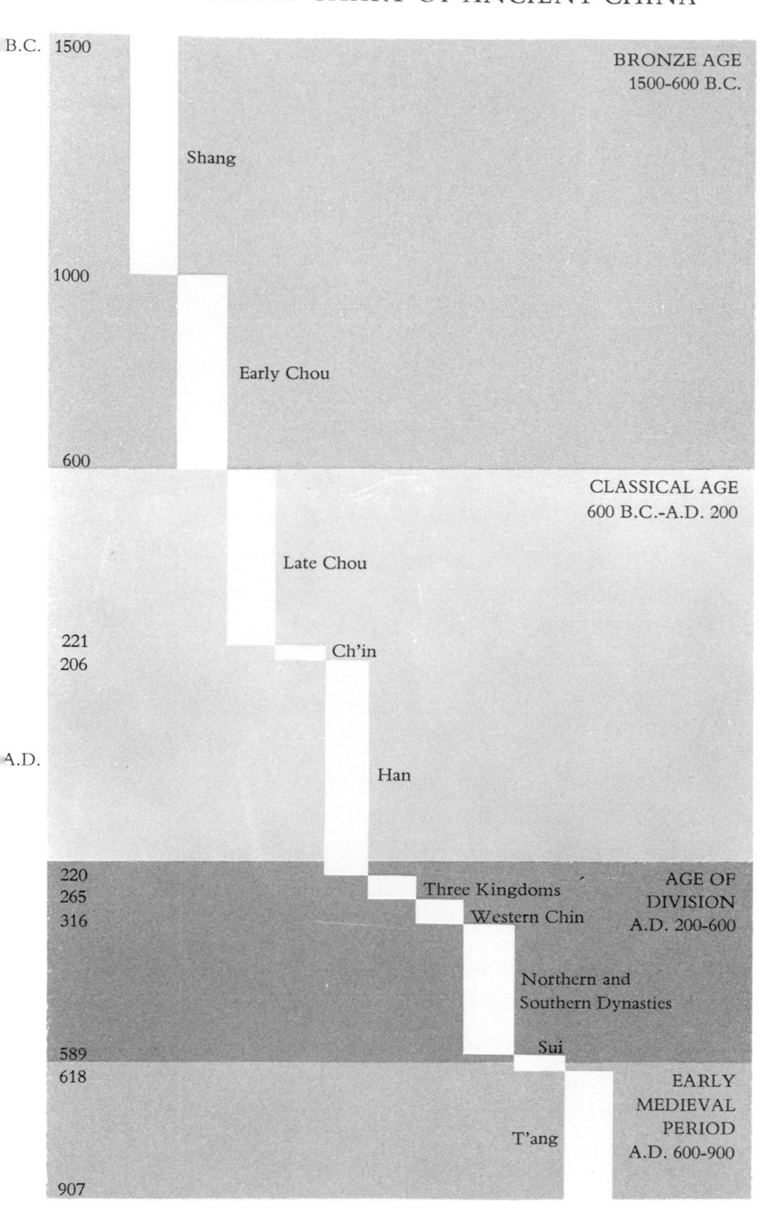

CHINA'S HISTORY *began about 1500 B.C., and during the following 2,400 years 10 major dynasties ruled the nation. On the chart at the left the yellow bars indicate the tenure of each dynasty; the horizontal bands divide Chinese history into four major periods.*

The vacuum left by the collapse of the classical social and political order and the virtual annihilation of the old nature-religions was gradually filled by two competing though mutually dependent systems of thought and belief. We know them today as Taoism and Buddhism.

Taoism first began to attract adherents from all levels of society towards the end of the Han era. Rejecting all rigid norms and accepted standards, the Taoists proclaimed the virtue of individuality, and decried all forms of compulsion, distortion and artificiality. They offered eternal life, not through striving, but through understanding of the secret processes of nature. Great numbers of hermits, revolutionaries and starving peasants were attracted by this prospect of salvation in the confused, unhappy times that followed the collapse of Han.

Simultaneously, another new faith appeared, this one coming to China from India. At first the toy of a few upper-class eccentrics, Buddhism soon became popular. First the petty barbarian States of the north, then the discontented Chinese of the south felt the lure of a gospel of escape from suffering proclaimed in its simplest form long ago by Buddha, a contemporary of Confucius. With this faith it was possible for a man to escape the pain and anxiety inherent in the human condition, either by the self-achieved realization that all worldly experiences are illusory, or else by the power of spiritual beings to bring a believer out of the deadly chain of reincarnations in this harmful world into a place of eternal peace.

Along with Buddhism's healing gospel and its hope of escape and eternal salvation came a whole new culture, to change the Chinese vision of man and the universe for ever. It included a great, complex paraphernalia of philosophy about the nature of human understanding and the character of the real but hidden world. It offered new and more rigorous disciplines of philology that gave the Chinese better insights into the peculiar qualities of their own language and its history. It even gave birth to novel ideas and techniques in medicine and astronomy, already well-developed sciences in ancient China. And the believer's need to renew his morals and understanding of the best sources led to the opening of new ways of communicating with the holy land of India, especially the sea routes over the great southern ocean, which were soon thronged with pious pilgrims.

A by-product of this era of contact with the outside world was the name China itself, which caught on in the Indian and Persian lands where a name like "Middle Kingdom" would have had little meaning. "China" seems to be an altered form of the name of the Ch'in Empire. Long after the fall of that renowned nation, its name remained current in several forms as the popular name for the Middle Kingdom among the nations of south Asia. But a native of Ancient China would have encountered that name only in reading translations of the holy books from India. And even then he might have had to seek a learned pundit's help to discover that the Chinese syllables *Chin-tan* represented "Chinastan" (i.e., "China-land"), a strange, foreign name for his own homeland.

Out of these centuries of ferment came the splendour of medieval civilization in the Far East, when China, finally known by that name, became the wonder of the world. The hallmarks of the house of T'ang, which ruled the reunified Middle Kingdom during the seventh, eight and ninth centuries A.D., were its prosperity, its freedom, its gaiety, its experimentation and its unique contributions to art, music, literature and gardening. It was an age of faith in which the old ways of thinking became thoroughly impregnated and altered by Buddhist beliefs and attitudes, just as early medieval Europe had been profoundly altered by Greek and Roman Christianity. It was a second imperial age, comparable of the age of Han, but much richer, more cosmopolitan and sophisticated. Finally, it was an age of security and confidence, supported by successful wars against such neighbours as the Korean peoples of the north, the Vietnamese peoples of the south and the Tibetans and Turks to the west. It was during this age that the T'ang empire became the colossus of Asia.

In their conquests the T'ang armies converted the monsoon coasts of the distant southern frontier, long claimed but little absorbed, into a truly Chinese land, safe for settlers and for the benevolent activities of the Confucian magistrates, propagators of Hua civilization. Even in medieval times these tangled forests and green shorelines—in our time thoroughly tamed, cleared and planted in rice—were only partly explored, and remained largely the haunts of aliens and infidels.

Still, it was greatly desired country. Here Persian merchant princes repaired their great seagoing vessels with the fine wood of the schima, a relative of the tough southern oaks. The hot hill-sides were covered with endless stands of cinnamon and camphor trees, from which came supplies for the medicine chests of the north. Camellias and tea, which are intimately related, grew wild there, and were becoming widely appreciated. The halcyon kingfisher provided iridescent turquoise feathers for the head-dresses of noble northern ladies; the dark patterning of rosewood attracted dealers in carpentry supplies, and the heavy scent of kanari lured the makers of incense for Buddhist temples.

The adventurous immigrant into the new tropical south of T'ang learned to eat bananas and tangerines and lichees, and made them familiar to his friends in the north; he learned to make furniture of the tangled liana vines of the forest, and brought back red and yellow hibiscus for his gardens. He seized green peacocks in their primeval roosts and sent their tail feathers north to become expensive fans, and he captured green turtles in the phosphorescent sea to make soup for royal banquets.

The vivid, vivacious and complex culture of T'ang—in which seemingly disparate and incompatible elements from many parts of the world and many levels of society were welded into a glittering whole—represents the climax of a civilization that we now identify as "Chinese". During the 12 centuries that separated Szu-ma Niu in his bronze-fitted chariot from the silk-robed, jade-belted T'ang rulers of much of Asia, China had developed intellectual, technical and artistic resources that made it both the Greece and the Rome of the Far East.

A KNEELING FIGURE, *cast some 2,500 years ago, is shown against a silhouette of its head.*

A GOLDEN AGE IN BRONZE

The Chinese, more than most people, have always looked back on their earliest years as the "good old days", a time when men were virtuous and life was at its best. Their view of that distant era relied more on fable than on fact, however, until this century, when archaeologists unearthed hundreds of objects made during China's first two dynasties, the Shang and Chou (1523 to 223 B.C.). Fashioned of bronze by master craftsmen, these treasures include superb figurines, ceremonial vessels and furnishings, which reflect, among other things, the reverence for nature and family that characterized China's earliest "golden age".

Photographs by Pete Turner

SACRIFICES TO ANCESTRAL SPIRITS

Among the ancient Chinese, particularly the aristocracy, ancestor worship was a way of life. It was believed that when a man died, his spirit lived on in the upper regions and influenced the fate of his descendants on earth. In order to invoke the blessings of these spirits, their descendants brought them offerings of food and wine in ritual vessels of richly ornamented bronze. In time of trouble or need, special prayers of invocations might accompany the gifts. Kings made the most lavish and frequent offerings to their godlike predecessors, often seeking favours for the whole community, such as success in battle or an abundant harvest. When the king himself died, servants and guards were sometimes sacrificed to attend him in the afterworld—a bloody practice that gradually went out of style.

A STUDDED CAULDRON *was used to prepare meat presented to ancestral spirits. The handles and legs are shaped like horned animals; the two creatures facing one another on the front are birds.*

A STORAGE JAR *(opposite), in which sacrificial wine may have been kept, had ring handles on its sides with fittings in the shape of monsters' faces, set in a band of stylized natural patterns.*

A SACRIFICIAL VESSEL, *used for grain or wine, is shown in four views. The flange running down the centre of each side is the nose of a monster mask; on either si*

he flanges pairs of knobs represent the beasts' eyes. These stylized creatures, probably meant to ward off evil forces, are often seen in the art of Ancient China.

THE GLORY AND SUFFERING OF WAR

The leaders of early Chinese society were continually carrying on territorial feuds with one another, or waging fierce campaigns against neighbouring barbarians. Equipped with bronze helmets, daggers, spears and axes, these ancient knights rode forth in chariots lavishly decorated with bronze fittings. Each vehicle was manned by a driver, a spearman and an archer. Behind the chariots came the foot-soldiers; they were almost invariably peasants who had been forced to leave their fields.

Ancient annals recorded the deeds of chivalry performed by knights, but folk-songs more realistically bemoaned the lot of the peasant. One song wistfully lamented: "Long ago, when we started, the willows spread their shade. Now that we turn back the snowflakes fly. The march before us is long, we are thirsty and hungry, our hearts are stricken with sorrow but no one listens to our plaint".

A FILIGREED DAGGER, *probably used for ceremonial purposes, is shown against the silhouette of an axe. Once attached to a handle so that it could be swung, the weapon is pitted from oxidation.*

A FANGED DRAGON, *curling ferociously, was probably an emblem adorning the war chariot of a lord. The open end of the figure may have held the tip of a pole bearing the owner's standard.*

SHAPED LIKE A RAM, *this lamp had a hinged back that swung over on the head, forming a bowl that held oil and a wick. In all probability, the small, ornamenta*

A SQUATTING BEAR *served as a table leg in a luxurious feudal palace.*

onze lamp was used in the everyday life of a prosperous Chinese family.

THE SACRED ROLE OF THE HOME

In Ancient China home and family were held in such high esteem that they were considered almost sacred. The wealthy took pride in furnishing their houses with fine objects like the bronzes shown on these pages, giving them the rich and reverent atmosphere of a temple or shrine.

Much of this reverence of the home was bound up in the emphasis on ancestor worship, and its outgrowth, filial piety. Each father recognized that one day he would be an ancestor, and only by training his children to revere him while he was alive could he be sure that his spirit would be honoured upon his death. The young obeyed their parents without protest, and even a wealthy lord, whose home might be staffed with many servants, would patch his aged father's robes with his own hands.

MIRRORS OF THE UNIVERSE

The ancient Chinese believed that if a nation were virtuous, Heaven would shower good fortune upon it. The people, it was thought, would be rewarded with a temperate climate, adequate rainfall and plentiful harvests. If, however, a society had strayed from virtue, it would soon be assailed by calamities such as droughts, floods and famines. Often these natural disasters were regarded as sure signs that the government was corrupt and that the collapse of the dynasty was imminent.

Out of this vision of the workings of nature, the Chinese evolved many symbols for their cosmic beliefs. Often these figures appeared on the backs of bronze mirrors, like those shown on the right. The mirrors, which were sometimes worn to protect people from evil spirits, were suspended from the waist on a cord that was threaded through the knob in the centre of the design. The square inscribed around the knob stood for the earth. The T-shapes at the sides of the square symbolized sacred mountains that were thought to hold up the heavens. The circles beyond these, which enclosed a variety of zodiacal signs, patterns, mythical animals and inscriptions, represented the edges of the universe, and the unknown beyond.

ORNATE BRONZE MIRRORS *bear myriad cosmological signs and symbols on their backs. In Ancient Chi*

se highly polished mirrors were used more often for magical than for practical purposes, and they were frequently buried in graves to provide light for the dead.

2

A LIFE OF EXTREMES

A HOUSE FOR THE SPIRIT *was assured the dead by a pottery model like this one, an elaborately painted copy of a manor house of Han times. Such funerary models provide invaluable clues to early Chinese architecture.*

The traditional components of ancient Chinese society under the supreme ruler were the great lords who governed the land in his name, the knightly gentry who populated their Courts and fought their battles, and the peasants who provided the necessities of life to all classes. Outside this class structure, and therefore hardly recognized as true men, were merchants, artisans and slaves.

For the aristocrats, both great and small, life could be a rich and splendid affair. But for the man at the bottom, life was poor and changed little. The nameless farmer, grubbing in the yellow earth, continued to labour in misery.

The *élite* always knew that they could not live without the farmer and believed that reasonable attention should be given to his welfare. But no one suggested that he should be treated with honour—he was a necessary instrument, to be kept in trim without pampering.

The peasant was seldom an independent farmer. Occasionally one government or another would give him a field of his own, but the arrangement was usually short-lived. When civil disorders and invasions by nomads from the north weakened the structure of society, strong feudal lords extended their control over nearly all the land, great manors grew unchecked, and the farmer was forced to become a tenant again, and sometimes even a serf.

Despite the poverty of his life down through the ages, there were some gradual improvements in the condition of the farmer. For instance, he got better tools. The horny-palmed peasant of the Bronze Age had only a wooden hand-plough (if he was lucky, it had a bronze share), a simple hoe and a reaping-hook. But a tenant of a feudal lord of the fifth century B.C. might own a plough with an iron share, and perhaps an old ox to pull it. With this equipment, farmers improved the soil so that it retained rain-water more efficiently, made better seed-beds and resisted weed growth.

Even in the disorderly age that followed the collapse of the Han empire there was produced a multitude of ingenious mechanical contrivances that reduced the labour of the more fortunate farmers and increased the yield of their lands. A mould-board was added to the plough, ox-drawn carts seeded the fields automatically, complicated harrows prepared finer seed-beds and water-powered mills made more flour with less human labour.

The peasant was not only the backbone of the Chinese economy, he was also the muscle of Chinese power: he grew the food and he also fought the battles. In war, as on the farm, his equipment improved as Chinese culture advanced.

The men who went into battle to extend the rule of the kings of Shang and early Chou times wore amour made of the hide of buffalo or rhinoceros and carried "compound bows", reinforced with horn and sinew, that shot arrows armed with points of bone or bronze. But their chief weapon in hand-to-hand combat was a simple halberd with a bronze blade. Somewhat later, in the fifth century B.C., soldiers were equipped with two-edged swords—usually of bronze, though some may have been of forged iron.

Soon after, when the Chou feudal States were fighting desperately among themselves for supremacy or survival, innovations in military equipment multiplied, many of them originating among the northern steppe-dwellers. Regular troops of infantrymen and cavalrymen became more important than the patrician charioteers who had borne the brunt of battle in earlier times. The new horsemen wore barbarian trousers and boots, Scythian caps and gilded belt buckles—all quite un-Chinese. Foot-soldiers along the northern walls now depended on powerful cross-bows with bronze trigger mechanisms, and many men carried pellet bows that shot vicious little slugs rather than arrows. Such soldiers as these made up the victorious armies of Han that subdued a considerable part of Asia.

Military equipment underwent little change after the collapse of the Han empire, when most warfare consisted of conflicts among little States whose chief weapons were chivalry and deceit. None the less, some new mechanical devices appeared then, such as magazine cross-bows and multiple *ballistae* —large, mounted cross-bows—which were useful in the siege warfare that was the order of the day in the fragmented realm.

A farmer who was conscripted for war had little hope of resuming his normal life. The ordinary militiaman could expect to bleed on the hot sands of the north-western deserts, or even—in civil wars —on the good yellow earth. Capture was no guarantee of survival. Victorious generals liked to enhance their reputation for ferocity and to chill the hearts of future enemies by the mass execution of prisoners. The first-century writer Wang Ch'ung reports that officers of the ancient State of Ch'in, which was eventually to conquer all China, buried alive 400,000 soldiers of a rival State.

With better luck, a soldier might become a farmer again, but not necessarily on his own land. After Han times, the practice of establishing military colonies on unstable frontiers became increasingly important, and seed, ploughs and oxen were supplied by the State. There, semi-professional warriors were expected to protect their farms and families against all invaders. But, in difficult times, they sometimes made common cause with their barbarian neighbours, with whom they often intermarried.

With the re-establishment of social order by the medieval T'ang Dynasty, the land and the people flourished, and the mighty rulers conscripted farmers' sons by the thousands to extend the rule of the emperor into the remotest parts of the continent. Their bones fertilized fields that their fathers had never imagined.

The T'ang armies could boast somewhat more efficiency and much greater elegance than their predecessors. Although the simpler soldiers still wore hide amour, and sometimes only breastplates of wood, felt or paper—the best soldiers were provided with iron-plate armour, sometimes gilded, or with the fine chain mail recently introduced from the Iranian west. But their weapons were not much

GUARDIAN OF A TOMB, *this ceramic warrior, armoured and ready with a sword, was buried with a well-to-do Chinese long before the T'ang Dynasty was founded in A.D. 618. The figure was placed in the tomb to ward off evil spirits and vandals who might violate the grave.*

changed. Bows were made of the resilient wood of the mulberry, or of the palmyra palm of the far south. Although some arrows were now tipped with steel, they were only improved versions of ancient missiles. Still, the best swords were far superior to the old ones. Their blades were made of steel that was strip-welded to make them exceptionally tough and give them a beautiful damascened appearance —a process learned from India, it seems—and their shagreen-wrapped hilts were decorated with gold, silver or rhinoceros horn.

For the privileged classes of Han and T'ang, military life offered excitement and danger under exotic skies. Aristocratic young Chinese officers, armed with their new weapons and clothed in brocaded gowns and hats of marten fur, left their wives and sweethearts to fight the nomads on the edge of the Gobi Desert. As described in a ninth-century poem:

They swore to sweep the Hsiung-nu away,
without regard for their own persons:
Five thousands of them, in sable
and brocade, lost in the Hunnish
dust!
Pitiful without a resting place—those
bones on the river's edge:
They are still live men in the
dreams of distant boudoirs.

Yet death on the battlefield was perhaps preferable to the lot of the captured, who, when spared execution, were almost always condemned to slavery. Despite occasional abortive attempts by humane monarchs to abolish the commerce in slaves, the institution of slavery itself was never loudly or effectively challenged. Prisoners of war were only one source of supply. Great numbers of slaves were Hua men. Some of them were whole families condemned for a crime against the State by one of their relatives; others were men who had been sold by themselves or their families to pay debts.

In T'ang times, thousands of nomads from Mongolia and Central Asia, captured in the wars with China, were used as horse-herds, grooms, falconers and outriders to the carriages of Chinese noblemen. A few of them—expert potters, weavers or musicians—might become the gifts of the emperor to great vassals and rise to substantial positions. Unskilled war captives were herded into the feverish jungles, where they died in droves working to make the land habitable for their Chinese masters.

Many female slaves were entertainers, the Chinese counterparts of the Japanese geishas. In Chou times, women were sold publicly to private persons, and there were also State courtesans whose talents were required at parties given by the great lords. By the ninth century, in the capital of Ch'ang-an, officials of the T'ang bureaucracy as well as young candidates for public office thronged the geisha quarters that were close to the national administrative offices. The girls themselves learned popular arts under rigid discipline; the most successful of them were not only beautiful and talented but also gifted in witty repartee. Some attracted the devotion of eminent personages.

More is known about the slaves and peasants of Ancient China than about the merchant class. The classical scheme of things did not acknowledge their existence at all. Traders and shopkeepers had always been viewed with mistrust by the privileged classes of China; the few merchants mentioned in Chinese literature are usually foreigners.

Merchants were allowed only a small, carefully supervised role in the transfer of everyday commodities. The finest and most expensive goods—glassware, drugs, gold and incense—were brought to the imperial Court by vassals of the ruler, or their emissaries, in the form of "tribute". This was balanced by reciprocal "gifts" from the emperor to the humble contributor. This elaborate system of trib-

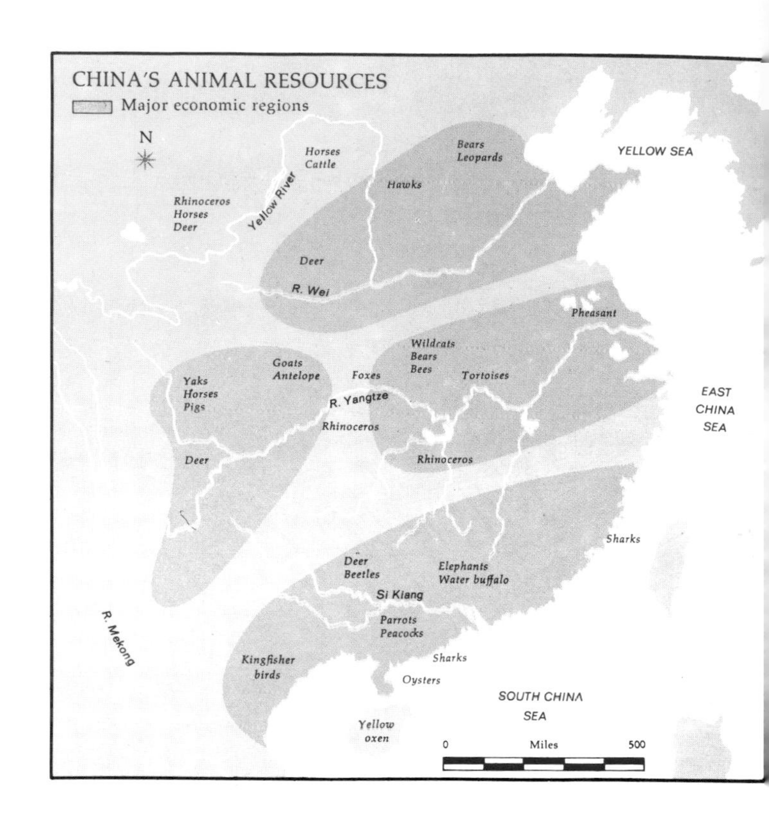

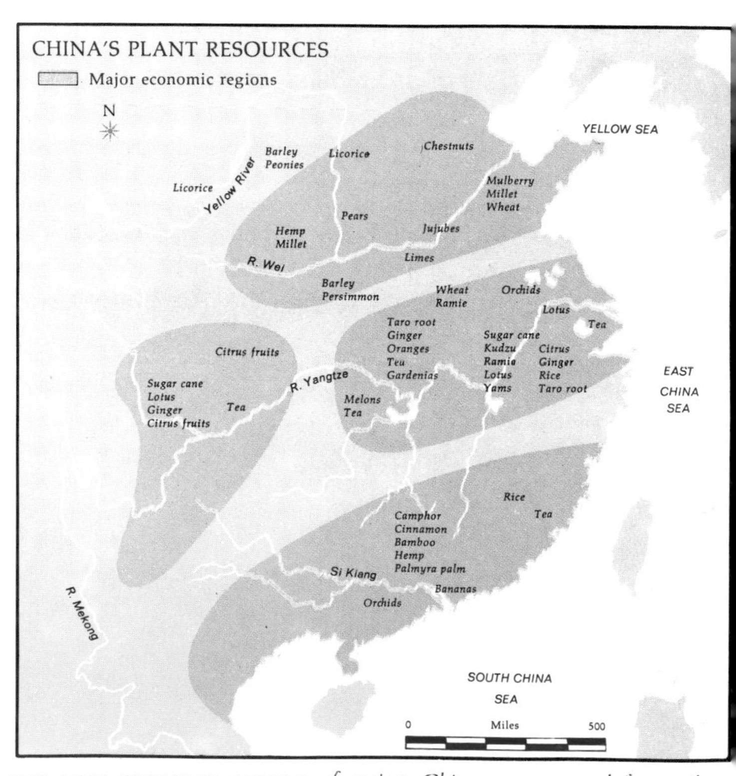

THE MAIN ECONOMIC REGIONS *of ancient China—reconstructed from tribute lists of the T'ang Dynasty—were situated in the Yellow and Yangtze river basins, in the west and along the southern coast. These areas produced such staples as rice, millet and tea, and a variety of animal hides and meat.*

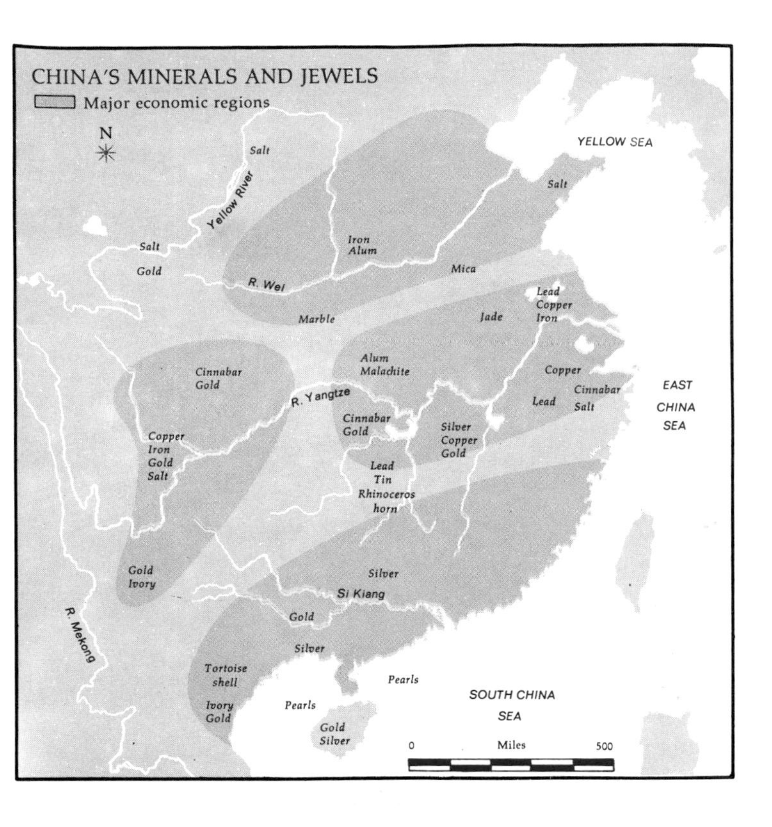

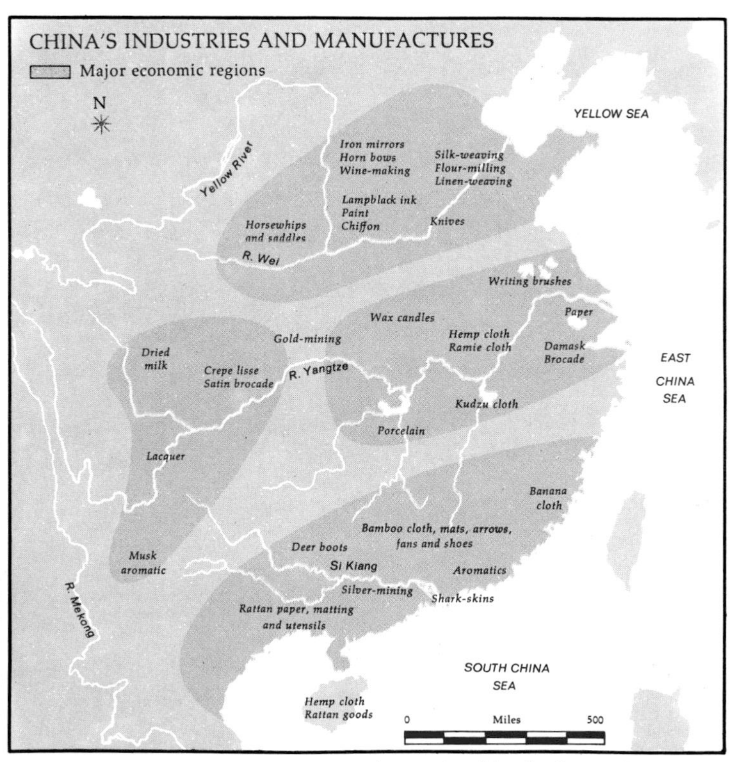

MINERALS AND MANUFACTURES *were also produced in the four main economic regions. Brought as tribute to the emperor by visitors were gold and silver from the south, and iron and salt from the middle Yangtze. From all four areas came silks or other fabrics woven of banana, hemp and kudzu fibres.*

ute to the emperor left no room for serious competition from the would-be entrepreneurs. As for basic products vital to the economy—such as salt, iron, wine and tea—imperial agents took charge of their production and distribution. Indeed, the salt and iron monopolies were mainstays of the imperial budget from Han to T'ang times.

We still know very little about ancient shops and shopkeepers, the purveyors of the many everyday necessities produced by farms and workshops for the common man. We are best informed about the great public markets of the medieval capital city of Ch'ang-an, which contained specialized warehouses and bazaars dispensing objects of bronze, leather, silk and wood, and were enlivened by street acrobats, story-tellers and every kind of strolling foreigner—Persian gem-dealers, Turkish pawnbrokers and many others. We hear frequently of drug shops, and of vendors of cakes and sweetmeats. There were places for relaxation with cups of tea or wine. But we do not know how one bought pickles or baskets or shoes.

The product most sought by the city shopper was millet, the grass cereal that had been the staple of Chinese diet since earliest times—Confucius must have subsisted chiefly on millet cakes and dried beef. Wheat and barley cakes became common later, and even a poor man might augment his meal with beans, turnips and melons, flavour it with onion, ginger or basil, and top it off with peaches, plums or persimmons. If a man were moderately well off, he might occasionally add a bit of pork or chicken to this menu. For settlers in the south, rice became the staple, and was supplemented by taro root, grown—like rice—in flooded fields. A poor peasant or a traveller in the drier southern uplands might occasionally eat yams. Subtropical orchards supplied tasty oranges and tangerines, and the adventurous new-comer to the south might steel himself to the strange flavours of bananas, sago, coconuts and stewed frogs. A characteristic feature of the Chinese diet, which seems to have developed mainly after Han times, was a preference for all kinds of pickles and preserves, as well as fermented sauces and relishes, based on fish, shrimps, meat and beans.

By medieval times new edible plants unknown to the classical age were added to the Chinese cuisine: spinach came from the far west, as did pistachio nuts; dill was brought in from Indonesia; almonds from Turkestan. There were hundreds of other novelties. The gourmets of T'ang had developed an appetite for flavours that would have repelled their simpler ancestors. Cultivated northerners prided themselves on a refined understanding of the properties of various kinds of native mushrooms and on a taste for odd country dishes, such as wine-marinated white carp and steamed shoats in garlic sauce. They ate dumplings shaped and flavoured like 24 different flowers, fluffy wheat steamed in baskets, "snow babies" made of frogs' legs and beans, and a kind of ice-cream—a chilled mixture of milk, rice and camphor.

The Chinese equivalents of the popular beers and wines of the ancient Western world were the fermented products of the home-grown cereals, especially millet and rice. All men, great and small, rejoiced in these beverages. But there were more exotic drinks: grape wine for the fashionable party; coconut milk for the refreshment of melancholy exiles in the tropical jungles; palm toddies to take the thoughts of southern administrators away from the threats of malaria and poisoned arrows.

The pleasures of wine drinking are alluded to frequently in Chinese literature. The great T'ang poet, Li Po, is famous both as a drinker and as a writer about wine. One of his poems expresses, in a humorous but slightly macabre vein, his concern for a recently deceased wine merchant, Old Lao. The old man descended to the "Yellow Springs" and the "Terrace of Night" under the earth, and Li Po, left behind in the land of the living, wonders if a customer comparable to himself can be found there:

Old Lao, down below in the Yellow
Springs,
Must still be brewing his "Great
Spring" vintage.
But without Li Po in that Terrace of
Night,
To whom can he be selling his wine?

During the unsettled post-Han age, China became familiar with a new non-alcoholic drink. Confucius never tasted tea, and it is doubtful that Wang Ch'ung, six centuries later, did either. The leaves of the tea plant, a close relative of the camellia, were first gathered in the warm south, probably by barbarians, to be brewed in water for a hot, strengthening drink. By T'ang times the novel beverage was becoming popular in the north, especially among the *élite* classes, and white and pale-blue porcelain teacups were being made for the tables of connoisseurs. Formalities grew upon formalities, and, by the ninth century, a stylized cult of tea preparation and drinking existed in most parts of China—as it still does in Japan today.

Beauty and formality are seen also in traditional Chinese costume. The *élite* had worn silk, made from the cocoons of the world's first domesticated silkworms, as long ago as Shang times. Simpler men managed with lesser materials, but the skilled Chinese made fine fabrics—almost as fine as silk—from woven vegetable fibres such as hemp, ramie, kudzu and banana.

The basic costume was established by the early classical period, the sixth century B.C., and consisted of a two-piece outfit—a long tunic, usually belted or sashed, topped by a jacket. The design was the same for all classes, but the materials and the refinements of detail varied in accordance with the wearer's position. For ritualistic occasions most men wore additional outer garments of mystic colours and symbolic patterns.

The men of classical China were particularly proud of their shoes, which distinguished them from barefooted barbarians. Peasants wore straw sandals, but the upper classes had fine cloth slippers—often of heavy damask or brocade.

At the end of the Chou period, in the third century B.C., this costume began to be modified by influences coming from the northern nomads. Underpants, leather trousers, leather shoes and leather belts with gilded and jewelled hooks in the vigorous "animal style" of the steppes became popular. By medieval times, other outside influences were reflected in further innovations; the ladies of T'ang were proud to appear in public in the latest Turkish and Iranian styles.

Hair style was particularly subject to the vagaries of fashion. The traditional men's head-dress was a simple hat or kerchief, but by T'ang times a topknot wrapping of some kind or a gauze cap stiffened with lacquer was popular. Men and women alike wore gold and gems on their heads—even men required elaborate hairpins to hold their topknots in place and the women balanced tinkling golden crowns decorated with pearls and precious stones.

Upper-class women owned little boxes with compartments, provided with mirrors, in which they kept their cosmetics. These included rouge, coloured with safflower or cinnabar, for their lips and cheeks, white lead or rice powder for their faces and shoulders, and blue, black or green grease for the manufacture of illusory eyebrows. Eyebrows were at all times subject to the whims of fashion: sharp-pointed tops were the vogue in the second century B.C. and curved arches in the second century A.D.; there were "sorrow brows" in late Han times and "distant mountains" in T'ang. Mouches appeared on ladies' faces at the end of Han; yellow foreheads had their heyday in T'ang.

In Ancient China, both peasant and king lived in the same kind of house. Even the most imposing buildings were only exaggerated farm-houses: a manor, like a farm, consisted of a courtyard with a gate in its south wall (the direction of holiness), a complex of buildings within the yard, a main dwelling in the centre and a garden behind. The number and kinds of buildings varied enormously from one courtyard to another, and of course the materials and the decorations of a royal palace or a holy temple were incomparably more elegant and durable than those of a farm-house. But the basic differences were slight.

From the earliest times the walls surrounding the house complex were made of rammed earth, and individual buildings were erected on rammed-earth foundations. The buildings were simple rectangular structures with roofs supported by rows of wooden pillars based on stone plinths. Spaces between the pillars were bridged above by horizontal timbers, and were usually filled in with plastered earthen walls. In the earliest times, roofs were made of thatch—the first roof tiles did not appear before Chou times. Wood was always the basic building material; stonework was used only on public and religious structures—for an occasional elegant pavement, balustrade, staircase, platform or burial chamber.

Chinese building techniques were conservative, and the innovations were minor; once introduced, however, they tended to become permanent. Among such changes were the elaborate sets of brackets that were developed in late classical times to support the long projecting eaves that had replaced the simple capitals topping the pillars of antiquity. By T'ang times, the shadowing eaves began to turn upwards in graceful curves—an architectural feature now regarded as typically Chinese.

The oldest of the great Chinese buildings—the pride of the Bronze Age—were decorated with images, probably religious or magical, done in red and black lacquer, which was then the chief medium of painting. By Han times the walls of important public buildings were painted with edifying scenes from the lives of the ancient sages and kings. Gilded pillars, window-frames adorned with bits of mica and coloured glass, vermilion rafters and marble staircases enhanced the beauty and dignity of upper-class houses of Han and later times. But the framework remained the same through the ages: a hall of wooden pillars and lintels set on a foundation of earth and stone.

The amenities inside the great houses became steadily more elaborate. Even after the fall of the Han Dynasty, during the age of division, a few rich and powerful men could instal unparalleled luxuries and conveniences in their homes. Consider, for example, the fantastic Court of Shih Hu, who reigned over the small northern State of Chao during these times. Shih Hu was a complicated man. He was a barbarian, a skilled archer and hunter, descended from some wandering shepherd from the northern steppes, yet his chief adviser was a learned Buddhist monk, and under his rule the gentle faith of Buddhism was permitted to flourish. He was a violent man—his given name "Hu" appropriately means "Tiger". In his splendid palace he had all-girl orchestras and battalions of female soldiers clad in sable furs, wearing golden rings and carrying bows painted yellow. Late in life he became very fat, and had to be carried to the hunt in a litter borne by 20 men. It contained a revolving couch from which he could shoot in any direction.

This ingenious litter was typical of the man, his capital city and his palace. It boasted a handsomely painted bath-house, where water spewed from the mouths of nine dragons into a great jade basin and drained away through the mouth of a bronze tortoise. Another building was equipped with air-conditioned summer rooms, cooled by ventilators connected to ice-storage pits. Among many mobile mechanical contrivances were a cart bearing a man-like figure that always pointed in the holy southern direction, and another surmounted by an image of the Buddha, which was constantly laved by water spurting from the mouths of dragons and scrubbed by a group of wooden monks.

By the ninth century, prosperous households in the capital city of Ch'ang-an were equipped with baths, heaters, mechanical fans, artificial fountains and ice-cooled rooms. In these times, the villas of some aristocrats boasted "pavilions with automatic rain", and one medieval emperor had a large hall that was completely air-conditioned. A favoured guest of the monarch's described a whirling fan that sprayed water behind the royal throne, from which blew a cool artificial breeze. The guest was invited to sit on a stone bench that was cooled from within, and he sipped an iced drink as he watched the curtains of water that fell from all four eaves of the building.

The typical house of a well-to-do T'ang family was decorated with furniture and accessories made of wood, metal, lacquer, glass and ceramics. Wooden articles included spoons and chopsticks of fine-grained jujube, writing brushes of bamboo, and perhaps a harp of paulownia wood. The family might own a bronze mirror, its back inlaid with amber and turquoise; ewers and goblets of hammered gold and silver; and dishes made of fine porcelain or blown glass. The favoured colours for these wares were the colours of the best jade—white, pale blue or green. A cultivated gentleman of the ninth century, admiring his teacups, would have remembered this sentiment:

Porcelain of Hsing is akin to silver.
Porcelain of Yüeh is akin to jade.

AN ANCIENT GAME, *called Liu Po, is played by two gentlemen while a servant looks on in this tableau of Han Dynasty funerary figurines. The rules have been lost to history but each player apparently used six pieces, which he moved around a board; the moves were determined by throwing six sticks.*

High-born Chinese ladies and gentlemen, waited on by corps of servants and slaves, whiled away their leisure in various entertainments. They enjoyed sports, parlour games, music and dancing, and the great seasonal and ceremonial festivals that marked such occasions as the new year—or the emperor's birthday. Some of these amusements were shared by the lowliest common folk. Hunting, for example, was a sport indulged in by everyone. A royal hunt was a grand affair, with beaters, dogs, cheetahs and eagles. But even a lesser nobleman might enjoy a day on the plains with a trained Korean falcon, and a commoner could take his goshawk into the forest with the hope of adding a hare or pheasant to the family pot.

There were other active sports, including a kind of football that had been popular since antiquity and that was regarded as a useful military exercise. In T'ang times, emperors, courtiers, scholars and even ladies enjoyed the game of polo, which had been introduced not long before from Iranian lands. Persian horses from Iran were in fact greatly prized in China by polo players, soldiers and sportive aristocrats. Brought to China in Han times when the Han armies opened the west, and attached to the emperor's stables to augment the royal herd of Mongolian ponies, Iranian horses had a special glamour and were known as "dragon horses" or "horses of heaven". T'ang poetry is full of allusions to them.

Among the less active sports were board and table games, some of which were distantly related to modern Parcheesi, lotto and backgammon. One very ancient and very popular board game now known around the world under its Japanese name of "go", had overtones of military strategy. Playing cards are also thought to be a Chinese invention of the T'ang period.

Dancing was inseparable from life, religion and all ceremonial acts. The ancient kings had danced to appease the drought demons of Shang times, and in the time of Confucius, troupes of barbarian dancers twirling yak tails and wands tipped with pheasant feathers performed in the Courts of the kings to drive away evil spirits. Some magical dances such as these were still being performed in the Courts of the emperors of T'ang, but, by medieval times, there were also dances that were performed purely for the entertainment of sophisticated audiences. The wild galops of the Turks and the Iranians delighted upper-class T'ang gatherings. Another extremely popular dance was the speciality of Sogdian twirling girls; they performed it on the tops of large rolling balls while attired in costumes of green pantaloons and crimson robes.

Music, an inseparable part of dancing, was at the same time considered a much more serious pursuit. The Chinese men had always believed that music had mystical and moral properties. Confucius and his followers held that certain kinds of music were elevating and purifying, while others led to corruption and depravity. Accordingly, music was put high on the list of required subjects in the education of gentlemen.

The most holy and venerable of musical instruments, revered perhaps even beyond the great bronze bells that rang in Court and temple, were sets of stone chimes—triangular pieces of limestone that were suspended in racks and struck with batons. These were sounded in the sacred orchestras of Shang, and were still being played in the classical ensembles of T'ang. Drums, bells and flutes were also ancient and respected instruments. Stringed instruments were less highly regarded, except for a certain kind of zither, the music of which was thought to be especially suitable to the meditations of respectable gentlemen. Harps and lutes, which became very popular after their introduction from western Asia in Han times, were generally used on informal, relaxed occasions. A unique instrument was the *sheng*, a kind of mouth-organ made by inserting a set of canes into a gourd; apparently it originated among the peoples of Indochina. It found its way to Europe in the 18th century and influenced the development of organs, harmonicas and accordions.

Music and dancing formed the core of the most colourful and exciting of all entertainments—the great palace-shows, such as might be given on the occasion of an imperial birthday. At celebrations of the emperor's birthday in the early eighth century, the festivities were enlivened by a troop of a hundred dancing horses adorned with rich silks and precious stones and metals. They danced with tossing heads to popular tunes played by the palace orchestra. On the same occasions there were also displays of the tricks of foreign magicians, musical performances by bands of richly dressed palace girls and parades of elephants and rhinoceroses.

In addition to such special national celebrations, there were the eternal but ever-changing seasonal festivals, made meaningful by ancient beliefs, in which the lowliest clodhopper could find occasions for joy and the reaffirmation of faith. The end of winter and the beginning of spring, for instance, signalling every sort of spiritual and physical renewal, each produced a series of festivals, including salutations to the local earth-gods and mating and fertility rites. The whole cycle of months had a corresponding sequence of holidays, such as the brilliant street illuminations during the first month. After the introduction of Buddhism in the first century, there were also outdoor spectacles, subsidized by the great monasteries of the major cities, portraying episodes in the history of that faith for the edification of the public.

These festive rites and gay celebrations, enjoyed by the people of all classes, were the bonds that crossed the division of society and united all Chinese into one great civilization.

FRONTIER LORDS AND PEASANTS

During the illustrious centuries of the Han Dynasty (206 B.C. to A.D. 220), daily life in China was recorded in bas-relief on tiles and stones made for the tombs of wealthy men. Some of these sculptures, like the large halberd-wielding figure on the right who guarded the tomb from evil spirits, had specific religious meanings. But many others, designed to entertain the deceased, were purely secular renderings of hunting and fishing, huts and palaces, soldiers and jugglers—all the men and occupations of a vigorous world. China under the Han was vigorous indeed. For the first time, the country was truly unified—a single, vast State, infused by a common culture. Even in the remote western region of Szechwan, district officials aped the manners of the imperial Court, and peasants built their homes and ploughed their fields in fashions that prevailed throughout China. The most extensive visual records of the period are the sculptured reliefs in Szechwan's tombs, and ink rubbings of these reliefs, like the ones shown on these pages, portray Han life with irresistible vivacity and truth.

THE HARD LIFE OF THE PEASANT

Szechwan was one of the most fertile regions of China, yet the lot of its common folk was generally difficult. The tranquil fishing scene on the right—a composition assembled from several different rubbings—gives little idea of a peasant's hard life. He and his family usually lived in a draughty one-room house with a tile roof, a dirt floor and no furniture. Half his crops went to the landlord who owned his fields and another large part to the government; to feed his family, he had to trap small animals and catch fish—and during some periods of the Han Dynasty, even the fish were taxed.

In hard times, a peasant's life was almost unendurable. During the first 200 years of the Dynasty, such disasters as droughts, floods and wars struck no less than 20 times, forcing peasants to sell their children into slavery, kill their babies because they could not feed them, and even resort to cannibalism. And at just such times of calamity the government often tried to replenish its own shrinking coffers by raising taxes—a practice that gave rise to the proverbial Chinese saying, "An oppressive government is more terrible than tigers".

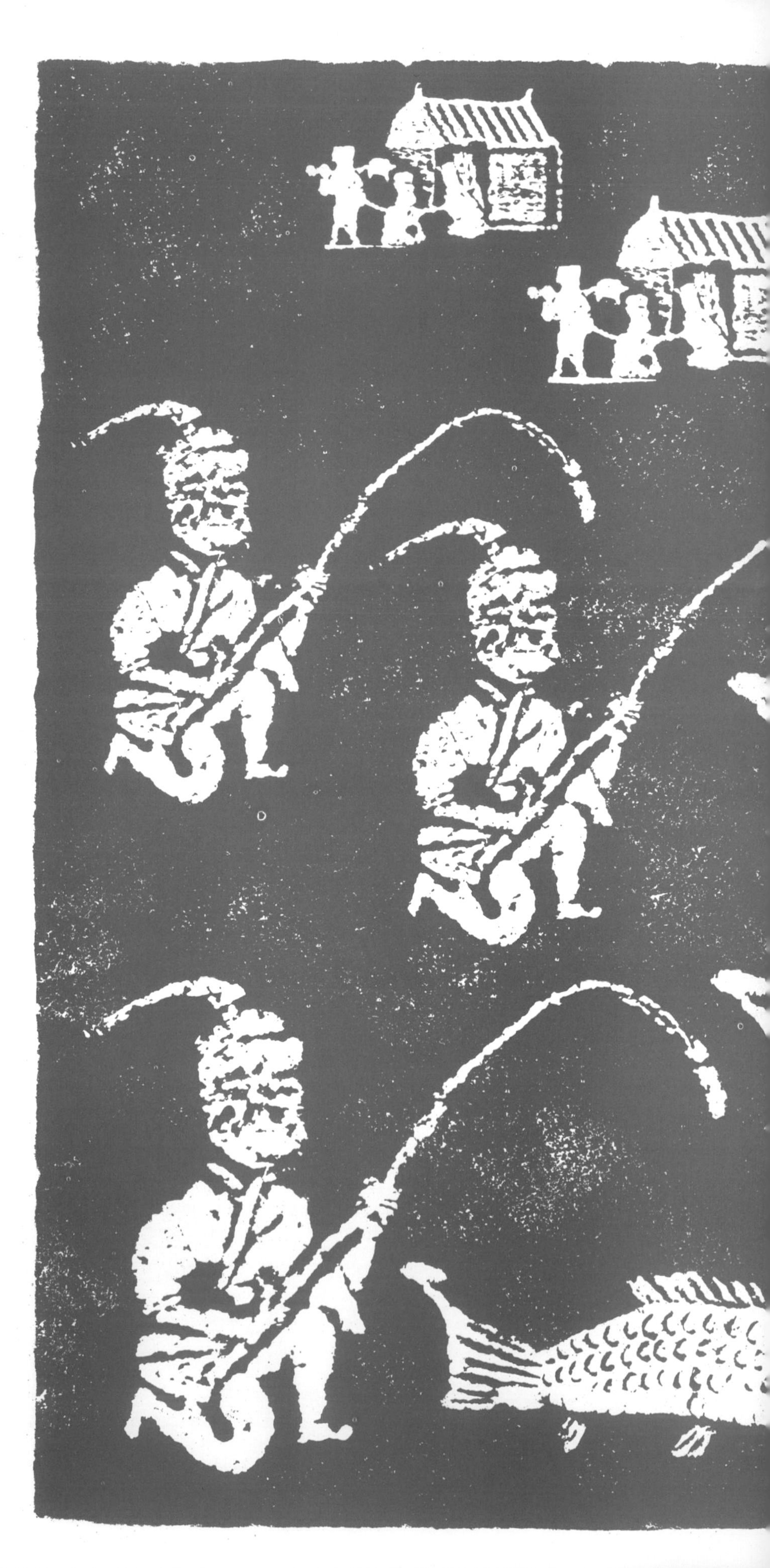

THE GENTLEMANLY SPORTS OF ARCHERY AND HUNTING

Archery was one of the traditional accomplishments of a Szechwan gentleman, along with writing, chariot driving and a knowledge of music and ceremonial etiquette. According to Confucian precepts, gentlemen displayed their skill as archers on three hunts a year, in the spring, autumn and winter. In this rubbing, two hunters draw their bows at a flock of geese overhead. Any sort of hunting must have been particularly rewarding in the Szechwan forests, for they abounded with quail and pheasants, foxes, deer and marmots. The gentlemanly hunter, however, never tried to bag too large a kill. If he used beaters to flush game, he placed them on only three sides, leaving the fourth side as an avenue of escape for the animals.

NOBLE STEEDS FOR THE EMPEROR

Harried relentlessly by barbarians from beyond its borders, the China of Han times was constantly at war. Lightning cavalry raids by the Hsiung-nu of the north were a constant threat. To repel such attacks the Chinese needed a sizeable cavalry, but years of civil war had decimated the nation's supply of horses. The supply was so low, in fact, that the first Han emperor could not in all his empire find four horses of the same colour to pull his chariot.

One great reservoir of horses to fill China's empty stables was Ferghana (present-day Turkestan), which raised magnificent steeds like those shown on the left. One Han emperor sent 60,000 men to Ferghana to seize horses by force, and married off one of his own female relatives to a barbarian king in exchange for 1,000 horses. Once obtained, these horses were bred at 36 stations in such frontier regions as Szechwan. Though the breeding programme eventually produced more than 300,000 horses, a good mount was still so valuable that it could be sold for 300 pounds of gold.

THE PRETENSIONS OF THE NEWLY RICH

Szechwan produced lacquered ware, brass utensils, dyes and silks, and its mines were a major source of salt and iron. Some men derived immense wealth by trading in these commodities. A really successful merchant rode in a cart with a coachman and an outrider (*below*), bought an honorary title from the emperor and built a mansion surrounded by gardens and pools. Such ostentation in mere commoners so infuriated officials and farmers that the government enacted laws against extravagance —at times it was illegal for commoners to ride in a chariot of any kind—and one writer denounced tradespeople who "neither plough nor weed", but "ride in well-built cars and whip up fat horses, wear shoes of silk and trail white silk behind them".

REVELRIES AT A FEAST

A large-scale feast was an occasion that brought all the Szechwan gentry together in an orgy of food and lavish entertainment. In fact, such feasts were so popular and disruptive that the government was forced to restrict them to holiday seasons; at all other times it was against the law to have more than three guests to dine.

Partly because feasts were so rare, the hosts spared no expense. They ordered the most exotic and expensive dishes—snails preserved in vinegar, dog-meat, turtles and slices of raw meat seasoned with ginger and topped with ant eggs. Troops of professional performers were hired to juggle and dance to the music of drums. Liquor was dispensed so freely that guests often rose from the audience and joined in the dances. Such behaviour led one poet to complain about unruly revellers who "keep dancing and will not stop", reeling about "with their caps on one side, and like to fall off". "Drinking", the author primly concluded, "is a good institution only when there is good deportment in it."

ARCHITECTURE FOR AN IMPERIAL AGE

No buildings erected during the Han Dynasty are still standing, but reliefs like the one on the right testify to their grandeur. The relief depicts a monumental gateway, flanked by memorial pillars and topped by tiled roofs and the figure of a mythological bird—the phoenix. In the early days of the Han Dynasty, architects concentrated on imperial palaces—perhaps because, as one builder explained, "without great size and beauty" the emperor's residence "would lack the means of inspiring awe".

But rich citizens soon rushed to imitate imperial splendour. They built sumptuous homes decorated with sculpture, paintings and costly draperies, and imported cashmere carpets. They even furnished family tombs with carved pillars and stone lions—and added inscriptions mentioning how much each item had cost. After the collapse of the Han Dynasty, several centuries of conflict brought a decline in architecture; but when China finally recovered, the new empire took the vanished glories of the Han as its models of magnificence.

3
HALLOWED WAYS

A POTTERY HEAD *with a painted animal-like mask, thought to represent a Stone Age shaman, is a relic from China's era of animistic religions. It adorns a lid that may have covered a funeral urn some 4,000 years ago.*

If a foreigner had come to the cosmopolitan Court of China in the eighth century A.D. and asked a gold-robed courtier, "What is the official Chinese religion?" the courtier would have replied, "The proper and seasonable worship of the gods of the mountains, rivers and seas and of our noble ancestors, as laid down in ancient books".

The origin of this religion goes back to prehistoric times when the earliest peoples of China sought answers to the same basic questions that have baffled primitive men the world over: what is the unseen force that brings darkness and light, winter and summer, drought and rain, life and death; what must man do to appease this force?

The men of Ancient China recognized the presence of this indefinable force. They believed that all things, even those that seemed to be inert, possessed it to some degree and that some things possessed it in outstanding amounts. It could be that a mis-shapen, moss-covered stone was full of this unseen force; there were also men who radiated a magnetic force as indefinable as that emanating from "holy" stones—they too had exceptional reservoirs of this power, concentrated in their blood.

In earliest times it was believed that this mysterious force was an integral part of the physical creature—it had nothing to do with disembodied spirits roving the air. To say that a tree stump contained spiritual power did not mean that it was the physical home of a ghostly being. It meant that the stump itself had an energy in it that could, in some mysterious way, affect other beings, like the electricity in a charged wire.

Gradually, personality came to be attached to elements of nature that appeared to radiate this spiritual power and that were close and familiar to a tribe. A "friendly" mountain that sheltered a settlement was believed to have the power to protect the settlement and was given a name; a local stream that appeared to the tribal leader in a dream and in which someone later drowned was believed to have the power to destroy and was also personified. In this way, the concept of the power of an unseen force began to find expression in the worship of individual nature-spirits.

To the Chinese tribes of prehistory and to the men of the Bronze Age, the era that began with the

THE RAIN SPIRIT *of the ancient Chinese was the dragon, the sacred symbol of the East and the "gatherer of clouds" whose beneficence was essential to a rich harvest. The bronze beast shown here is thought to be a lamp dating from the Han Dynasty.*

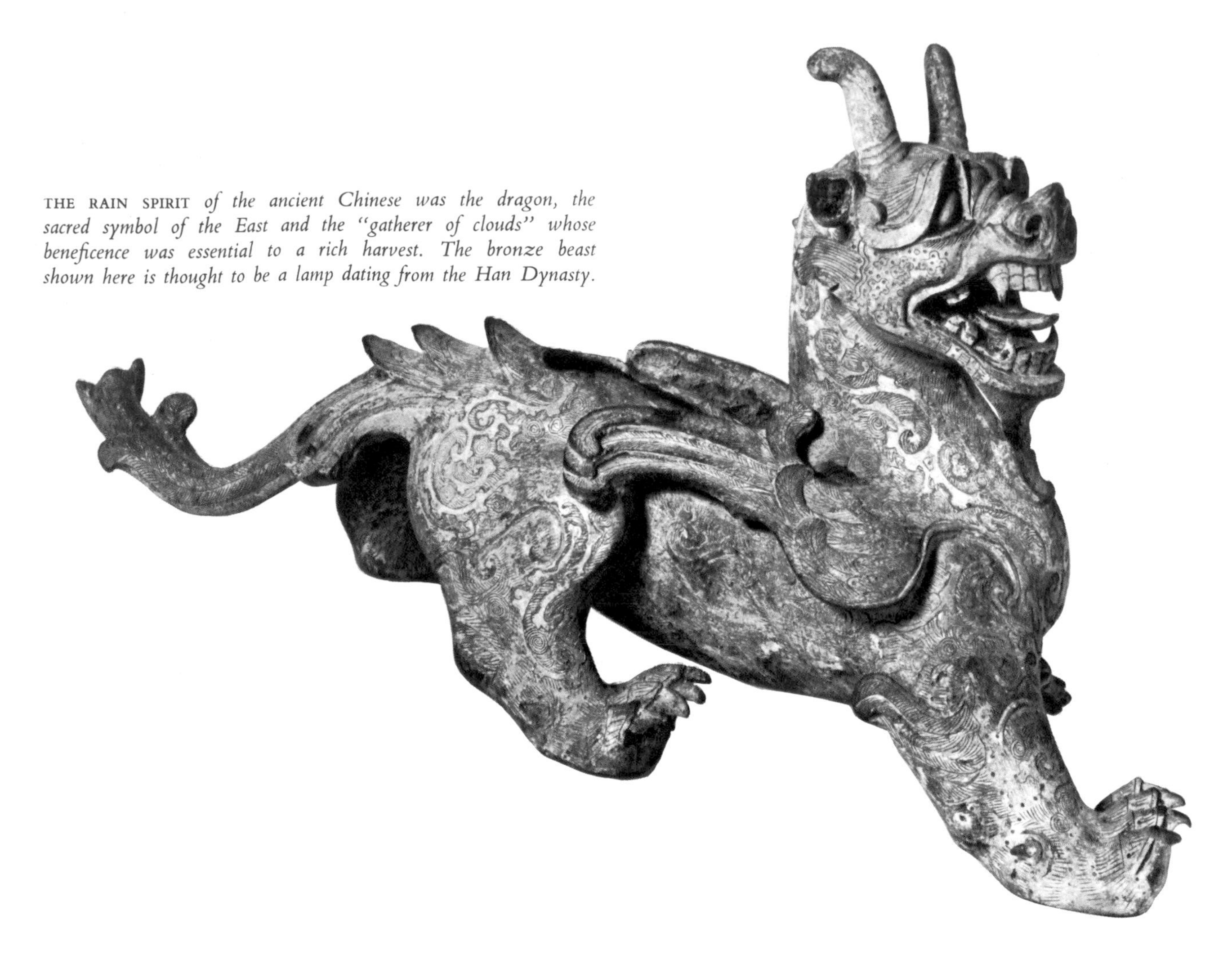

Shang Dynasty some 3,500 years ago, the great deities were those nature-spirits who inhabited the dominant features of the landscape. Hill-gods, earth-gods, river-gods, sky-gods, wind-gods, thunder-gods were created when the abstract power inherent in them became so evident that men recognized it and gave them names. In time these gods ranged from the simplest forest-imps and river-maidens, whose good will was sought by villagers and travellers, to the gods of the cloud-gathering mountains, worshipped by the king himself.

One of the oldest and certainly the greatest of the deities was the sky-god T'ien. In the very early days T'ien was thought of as a great king in the sky, more magnificent than any earth-bound king, more brilliant and more terrible. Later, many viewed him as an impersonal dynamo, the source of the energy that animated the world.

Among those in the next rank of nature-deities was—not unexpectedly—the "Sire of the Ho", the god of the Ho, or Yellow river. At regular intervals this mighty lord was offered a human sacrifice, a richly clad girl who, with a raft for her bridal bed, was floated out into his wet domain, never to return. An ancient hymn to the "Sire of the Ho" describes his palace of fish scales and cowries, and then the sacred ceremony:

You mount a white turtle, Oh!
your train is striped fish!
I rove with you, Oh!
by the aisles of the Ho.
In the chaos of a sweeping thaw, Oh!
down we shall go.
We join our hands, Oh!
as eastwards we move.
They escort the lovely one, Oh!
to the south estuary.
Waves in steady surges, Oh!
come to welcome us—
Fish, in swishing tumult, Oh!
are bridesmaids to me.

The world of spirits also included another class of potent beings; ghosts, the spirits of former kings and heroes as well as the helpful souls of one's own humble ancestors. They too had mysterious power and could have great influence on the welfare of the living. Ordinary ghosts were generally called *kuei*, meaning originally "effigy, puppet, strange or fearful manlike creature". The souls of some important men, however, achieved a higher spiritual status so that they could hardly be distinguished from the gods of nature, since a human soul might become the protective god of the field, the grove or the stream over which he had watched in his lifetime.

In all, there was a vast multitude of spirits who had to be noticed and appeased, and all Chinese, from the peasant planting his crops to the king planning a battle, depended on the wisdom and good will of the nature and ancestor gods. Proper communication between living men and these exalted spirits was by prescribed ritual that, if properly performed, was believed to bring about the well-being of all.

Basic to this ritual was contact with the world of spirits through a shaman—or rather a shamaness, since most mediums in Bronze Age China were female. The shaman is familiar to us as the medicine-man of primitive tribes, the medium whose spirit-possessed body speaks divine wisdom to common men. The shaman, whose chief function in arid northern China was to bring rain, did not supplicate the deity like a priest; he was believed to be physically but temporarily occupied by the deity who descended from his home beyond the clouds to visit the world of men. In a trance or paroxysm, the shaman spoke with the voice of the spirit and danced to bring rain. An ancient shamanistic chant describes such a holy woman—sweet-smelling and clad in a splendid ritual dress—welcoming the God of the East as a mistress welcomes her lover:

Bathed in hot orchid water, Oh!
hair washed in perfumes!
Dressed in many floral colours, Oh!
like the best of blossoms!

Other religious practices reflected in their violence man's terror of the unseen forces at work in his world, powers that were close to the sources of life and death. The worship of the spirits in ancient times was by no means a matter of polite ritual performed by literate mandarins with engaging manners. Knightly mourners screamed and leaped by the biers of deceased friends to drive harmful ghosts; shamans were burned publicly to bring rain to drought-stricken fields; women danced naked to exorcise unwanted dragon-spirits.

Most dramatic were the blood sacrifices, which are very old in China as they are elsewhere in the world. The animals and servants sacrificed at the tombs of the Bronze Age lords gave their blood, which was believed to contain the mysterious spiritual power, to their dead ruler, and in this way they gave him life. Holy bells and swords were consecrated by pouring life-giving blood on them, and the sanctity of feudal oaths was confirmed by smearing blood on the lips of a juror.

These primitive beliefs and ancient rituals were superficially modified with the refinements of human sensibilities during the Classical Age—the era of Confucius and other itinerant sages—that began around 600 B.C. Some of the gory but venerable customs assumed a civilizing gloss or passed from accepted upper-class practice into the shadows of ill-recorded peasant custom. With the fall of the Chou Dynasty some 300 years later, the identity of many of the early gods disappeared. But while some of the savage gods of the earliest peoples appear to have vanished, these too may have continued to live on in the faith of the common people, ignored by the literate class.

In the third century B.C., the powerful rulers of the newly established Han Dynasty began to organize an official State religion based on the centuries-old tradition of worship of nature-gods and ancestral spirits. This official cult was set up to ensure the power of the emperor and his appointees over the vast populace of a rapidly expanding empire. To avoid "irresponsible" interpretations of the wishes of the great gods of antiquity—interpretations that might disagree with imperial policies—a system of officially approved worship defined the true gods and appropriate rituals.

The gods of the Han Court ranged in dignity from the gods of the Five Directions—North, South, East, West and Centre—down to a miscellany of nature-spirits, believed, not always correctly, to have been worshipped in earlier times. The State cult of Han was conceived as a revival of the good rituals of the past, but, in fact, it was a composite and artificial system in which old gods hobnobbed with the young ones and almost forgotten provincial deities were given new and universal honours. Private communication with the gods through a shaman was discouraged and sometimes prohibited; even in official circles the use of shamans was reserved for occasions of extreme peril.

This State religion was artificially connected to a body of moral doctrine and beliefs thought to have been approved by Confucius. What the State religion actually had in common with Confucian ideas was respect for the good old days and for the ancient values said to have been endorsed by the founding fathers of Chinese civilization. But the antiquity of many of these beliefs was counterfeit.

The so-called Confucian classics were, in fact, compiled long after the death of Confucius by disciples of his disciples, and were edited and interpreted in Han times by government scribes; but they purport to reflect the views of the great sage

A WANDERING SAGE, *Confucius taught the value of proper manners and filial piety, and preached that kings were responsible for the public welfare. Though not widely recognized during his lifetime, his ideals lastingly influenced the culture of China.*

of antiquity on history, religious rites, morals and standards of behaviour. The State officers of Han times accepted these interpretations and associated them with the standardized pagan nature-worship of the State cult as a part of the acceptable way of life for a Han gentleman. We in the West sometimes call this way of life, which includes both reverence for the "ancient" books and the "ancient" gods, "Confucianism".

The most important text through which Confucian ideas were linked to the State religion, a compendium called the *Analects*, purports to be a record of some of the dialogues Confucius had with his pupils. The Confucius of these conversations emerges as an advocate of the practice of ritual for its own sake, whether it involved conduct in Court or conduct in a temple. According to the *Analects*, Confucius himself "sacrificed to the gods as if the gods were present", but when someone asked him about the significance of an ancient State ceremony, he confessed, "Truly, I do not know". A lover of ancient things, he believed that it was important to preserve old rituals because the practice of the rituals had its own value.

Thus the State religion, based essentially on the ancient gods and rites, is Confucian only in the sense that its form had been prescribed by the interpreters of books associated with Confucius and his age, not because Confucius founded it or was considered its chief deity. In fact, in his own time, Confucius had seemed to some men merely a loquacious bumbler, a self-serving pretender to exclusive understanding of ancient wisdom. An anti-Confucian polemicist wrote of him:

> *He eats without tilling, dresses without weaving. Wagging his lips and clacking his tongue, he presumes to be a source of Right and Wrong in order to delude the masters of Under-Heaven.*

In his own lifetime, Confucius had been only one of many itinerant wise men; in Han times he was regarded as an authority on customs and morals and it was almost inevitable that he, like other heroes, should later be deified. By the first century A.D. an irregular worship of Confucius, not very different from that accorded to local heroes, gathered momentum. In time, the master was known to all as a divine being whose coming had been foretold by miracles and whose worship was approved, along with that of some other great men, in the official calendar of gods.

The official Confucian State religion organized and maintained by the national government in Han times was considered to be responsible, controlled and temperate, while the remnants of the folk religion that did not fit into the State plan were thought of as irresponsible, uncontrolled and intemperate. Local cults were ruthlessly exterminated and temples of wayside gods were destroyed; all religious authority was focused in the capital city and all unorthodox belief was treated as mere superstition. It was the regular duty of officers of the State to destroy manifestations of the popular cult, but this policy was never wholly effective. Popular religion had grown out of the primitive roots of ancient folk belief, and the common people secretly continued to turn for assistance to such favourites as the pig-like thunder-gods, the slippery fish-deities and the brutal forest-trolls.

At the same time as the government scribes were consolidating and standardizing ancient beliefs, some of the upper-class *élite*, including Liu Ch'e, the great Han emperor of the second century B.C. (also known as Wu Ti), became deeply immersed in the body of esoteric doctrines, practices and pursuits that we call Taoism.

This many-faceted system had grown out of the same folklore and tradition as did the tribal and

A KEY TERM *in Chinese religions, the word "tao", or "way", originally meant simply a road or path. The character for it was a composite made up of parts representing movement (grey) and a head (black), symbolizing a man's direction. To Confucianists "tao" came to mean the ethical way, to Taoists the way of nature.*

liturgical tradition of "Confucianism". But the selection and emphasis of each were different. The Taoists maintained the shamanistic way, preferring to preserve the intimate relationship between those Under Heaven and their gods. They rejected the priestly hierarchy of the bureaucratic Confucian magistrates and their rigid and confining approach to the divine world.

The word "*tao*", after which this body of belief is now named, means literally the way, or the path; figuratively it can mean basic way of life or underlying order of nature. The Taoist use of the term emphasized the latter.

The most revered Taoist book is a poetic but obscure work called the *Lao Tzu*, which was claimed by the Taoists as their own because they saw in it certain fundamental concepts that were congenial to their ideas. The *Lao Tzu* pictures the *tao*, the way, as a great inexhaustible womb, the origin of all individual beings and experiences:

The Way is an abyss:
however you may use it, it needs no filling.
A gulf, Oh! seemingly the ancestor of the Myriad Creatures!
Fathomless, Oh! seemingly it will endure.

The second great Taoist classic, the book called *Chuang Tzu* is said to be the work of a Chou Dynasty sage named Chuang Chou and is less enigmatic. It is full of delicately conceived allegories emphasizing flux, metamorphosis and the interchangeability of life forms:

Long ago, Chuang Chou dreamed that he was a butterfly. He was elated as a butterfly—well pleased with himself, his aims satisfied. He knew nothing of Chou. But shortly he awoke and found himself to be Chou. He did not know whether as Chou he dreamed he was a butterfly, or whether as a butterfly he dreamed he was Chou.

The great aim of all Taoists was to conform to the way of nature. They believed that all attempts to behave in accordance with strict codes of discipline, either personal or governmental, were artificial and tended to deform human nature and thereby waste life. Their aim was to enhance vitality and life and ultimately to create a new, refined and immortal body that would leave the mortal body to take part in the bliss of paradise.

This longing for supernal life led to a great popularity of alchemists and magicians in the Han capital cities. These wonder workers streamed to the Courts and were welcomed because it was believed that those who had the power to refine crass material substances must also have the power to create the changes needed to make man immortal.

They brought with them a complex symbolism based on red, their holy colour, which represented the furnace of the alchemists and its beautiful, red-garbed patron goddess. One of their colourful symbols was their sacred bird, the Manchurian crane, with the red spot of divinity on its crown. Most important was cinnabar, a red compound of mercury and sulphur that was believed to have magic powers because it could be turned into a silvery liquid and then back to a solid; some even believed that it could be turned into gold, the one substance known to be indestructible.

The Han Taoists also prescribed various practices to strengthen life essence—yoga-like gymnastics, magic elixirs prepared by alchemists, and dietary rules, such as the avoidance of cereals. The first-century philosopher Wang Ch'ung described Taoist practices in this way:

> *They dose themselves with the germ of gold and jade, eat the finest fruit of the purple polypore fungus. By eating what is germinal their bodies are lightened, and so they are capable of spiritual transcendence.*

A being who had attained, by whatever means, this state of "transcendence" was called a *hsien*, a word that connotes taking flight from the material world, breaking mortal bonds and escaping spacial restrictions. The immortal *hsien*, similar to angels, were popularly styled "feathered folk", and their winged or feathered images appear in the art of the period. The book of *Chuang Tzu* pictures them as delicate, white-skinned superbeings:

> *These are divine persons dwelling there, whose flesh and skin resemble ice and snow, soft and delicate like sequestered girl-children; they do not eat the five cereals; they suck the wind and drink the dew; they mount on clouds and vapours and drive the flying dragons—thus they rove beyond the four seas.*

In late Han times, Taoism spread from Court circles and became a popular revolutionary cult, known as Yellow Turban Taoism; it promised immortality to ordinary men. The revolutionaries led by three rebels, the Chang brothers, attempted to overthrow the Han Dynasty and establish a Taoist State. Hundreds of thousands of destitute peasants flocked to their banner and joined the strange Taoist church that they established and made attractive to common men. Great mass ceremonies were held in which incense and music established the atmosphere for public confession of sins, prayers for other sinners, holy exaltations and sometimes uninhibited orgies. This army of exalted salvationists was a major factor contributing to the fall of the Han empire; but soon afterwards the movement disintegrated. However, Taoist speculation on transcendental matters remained a way of life for a growing number of educated recluses and anxious aristocrats. In the age of division that followed the collapse of Han it attracted a great many refugee intellectuals. They flocked to the south, and in this warm, genial environment developed their love of nature, poetry and landscape painting, all reflecting Taoist concern with the natural world and the important truths about eternity that may be found in it.

Between the third and the sixth centuries, when China was torn by internal strife and the northern area was overrun by hordes of barbarian nomads, centralized government could not survive. With the collapse of the bureaucracy came the fragmentation of the "Confucian" State religion that had been so closely linked to it. Taoism, in spite of its temporary popularity, could not by itself fill the void left by the disintegration of the classical society of Han. Into this vacuum poured the riches of Indian Buddhism, a religion whose chief aim was the elimination of human suffering.

Buddhism is named after its reputed founder, an Indian prince of the sixth century B.C. who came to be known as the Buddha, a word that signifies the Enlightened. The official story tells that the Buddha was a rich and pampered youth, who, aghast at the sight of suffering and death, sought and found escape in a belief in the illusory nature of the world. He preached that man's attachment to things, to possessions, to worldly hopes of every kind was all in vain—man loves that which does not truly exist and suffers when these things slide like sand between his fingers: "Each and every entity that has being is like a dream, an illusory bubble or shadow—it is like the dew, and also like the lightning". Once freed from desire and from attachments to material things, man could achieve the condition called "nirvana" and abandon the final illusion—the belief that the ego, the individual personality, is a real entity.

Such ideas appealed to some Taoists who themselves thought that all sensations and experiences were misleading. Accordingly, when Buddhism, enriched by its passage through the Graeco-Indian and Graeco-Iranian civilizations of Afghanistan and Central Asia, entered the Middle Kingdom in late Han times, Taoism took the foreign teaching under its auspices. Some early devotees of Buddhism regarded it as an exotic form of Taoism and the Buddha as identical with the supposed author of the *Lao Tzu*. In fact, according to one Chinese legend, he had travelled to India centuries before and founded the Buddhist faith. Even technical Buddhist terms were translated from Sanskrit, the sacred language of India, into traditional but misleading Taoist expressions; for example, *bodhi*—Sanskrit for "Enlightenment"—became *tao*, meaning "the Way".

Chinese Buddhism would probably have remained an exotic form of Taoism if it had not been for the constant intercourse between China and India maintained by devoted Buddhist monks, who, like Christians on pilgrimages to Rome or Jerusalem, renewed contact with the pure source of doctrine. During the age of division and invasions following the collapse of the Han Dynasty, the Buddhist schools of thought multiplied, and their monasteries filled the land—refuges for the dispossessed, quiet sanctuaries for the wise and hide-outs for tax evaders and escaped slaves. Pious aristocrats gave the institutions golden statues and large tracts of land, and gradually the monasteries acquired their own battalions of slaves, their own water-mills, their own shops.

In southern China emerged the important offshoot of Indian Buddhism known as Ch'an, and later as Zen in Japan. Its great leader in the seventh century was Hui-neng, a native of the far south and one of the first great men of China not of Hua, or Middle Kingdom, birth. His superiors once called him a barbarian, an allegation he did not deny, but his blunt and rugged personality and his willingness to speak directly to despised and rejected men were never forgotten. His sect laid little emphasis on the study of books and the uses of reason; he preached that release from illusion could come suddenly, even to an uneducated man. Through him, Buddhism became a light to the non-Chinese heathen.

In the seventh century, China was reunified under the great medieval dynasty of T'ang, and with the return of a strong central government and a huge bureaucracy came once again an official State religion, a Confucian cult that was very similar to the official religion established in Han times. Although the State religion was once again dominant, now there were Taoism and Buddhism to complement it.

By T'ang times, Confucianism, Taoism and Buddhism became known as the Three Doctrines. Although some thinkers held that they were basically the same, especially in their views of the spiritual destiny of man, the emphasis was still different in each.

Confucianism, the T'ang official cult, was conservative, like the State religion of ancient Rome, and emphasized man's duties to his fellow man and to his gods. An official account of eighth-century State ritual still survives and tells us plainly who were the great gods of the T'ang pantheon—the spirit-kings who controlled events in human society and its natural environment. They were, first, the gods of Heaven and Earth, not too clearly defined, but the great sources of being. Second came the ancestor-gods, particularly the divine ancestors and deified patriarchs of the reigning Li family. The chief star-spirits were third in order; they were the focuses of metaphysical power and determined the destiny of each region of T'ang and the fate of its human inhabitants. Fourth were the spirit-overlords of the greatest mountains, rivers and seas—the bony skeletons and the rushing arteries of the world, infused with divine energy. Typical of this class of deities was the newly elevated God of the South Sea, who presided over the sea that led from Canton to the Indies and beyond, bringing the wealth of many nations to the world of T'ang. His temple stood on a windy coast some distance from Canton. There, attended by swarms of wriggling sea creatures, he was offered vegetables, cereals, dried meats, salt and libations of wine as the local magistrate honoured him on behalf of the distant emperor in the capital of Ch'ang-an. After such gods came the lesser gods of mountains and waters and finally the spirits of inferior stars, mounds and barrows.

Even in medieval times the official cult continued to reflect some of the most ancient rites of the nature-religion on which it was based. During an eighth-century drought the archaic rain dance, which has antecedents traceable to the beginnings of Chinese history, was performed; clay images of human beings were exposed to the hot sky, replacing the living scapegoats of antiquity. In this same period, a high government minister sent shamanesses to perform religious rites in all parts of the realm. One of them was exceptionally beautiful and kept a Court of several dozen young men. She and they were put to death by an over-zealous local official who, it seems, did not relish this revival of the ancient wise-woman.

In times of stress, even the most barbaric of the old customs reappeared. When a great religious edifice was rebuilt in the city of Loyang, it was widely rumoured that a boy had been buried alive in its sacred precincts so that his spirit might guard it against malign influences. When a meteor fell over the capital city, terrified citizens whispered that bailiffs were collecting human livers to placate the dogs of Heaven. One of the great rebel leaders of T'ang times cut out the heart of a royal princess and offered it to the spirit of his dead son. Such barbaric aspects of the old nature-religion were never entirely lost.

While Confucianism stressed the efficacy of ancient ritual in determining man's fate, Taoism emphasized the search for immortality through man's understanding of nature, and few men of T'ang times were uninfluenced by this dream. Many medieval Chinese, some of them in high places, worshipped the legendary author of the *Lao Tzu* and devoted themselves seriously to the search for immortality and exhausted their resources in purchasing expensive reagents for the manufacture of elixirs. Even emperors, who served as heads of the official Confucian religion, honoured Taoist books and practices.

Midway in his 44-year rule, Li Lung-chi, the greatest of the T'ang emperors (known also as Hsüan Tsung), came to believe in the Taoist hopes for a harmonious natural life and for the penetration of nature's secrets. He gave new honours to Taoist gods and sages, especially to the supposed author of the *Lao Tzu*. Once he had a vision in which the latter appeared to him and told him where to find a true likeness of his countenance. The holy image was indeed discovered and made the basis of replicas that were installed in government temples throughout the realm.

So inspired was Li Lung-chi by Taoist belief in the sanctity of life, that he tried to abolish capital punishment and initiated measures for the humane treatment of animals. He also established an official examination in Taoist philosophy for the title of "Master of Mystic Studies", which led to important positions in the government bureaucracy.

As Li Lung-chi grew older, the mysteries of Taoism absorbed him more and more. Possibly this intense preoccupation led to visions, for he once told his ministers that, while burning incense at a private altar, he had been wafted up to Heaven. None the less, his fervent belief resulted in a great improvement in the reputation of the ancient books of the Taoist faith and in preservation of the arts of natural living that Taoism cultivated.

Closely related to the Taoist dream of immortality was the Buddhist doctrine of salvation. It maintained that man's hope lay in his understanding that ordinary experience is mere illusion, a doctrine that led many men to leave the everyday world for the serenity of monastic life. By medieval times Buddhist monasteries filled the land and even powerful statesmen and learned scholars made prolonged visits to these great centres of holiness.

The chief monastery in the capital city of Ch'ang-an in the eighth and ninth centuries was populated by monks "as numerous as blades of grass". Its grounds were planted with pine trees full of spiritual power; its serpentine pond was beautified by sacred lilies; it owned many relics of great antiquity, rare images of the Buddha in jade and sandalwood and great libraries of holy scriptures conserved in lacquered cases.

But the Buddhist faith had its enemies who opposed it as an exotic, anti-Chinese fad and who saw its monasteries merely as tax-exempt estates tying up great wealth in gold on the skins of holy images. This view led to spasmodic persecutions; in the ninth century, holy images were ruthlessly melted down and rare books were burned without mercy. Although Buddhist power waned, its compassion and charity—manifested in hostelries for pilgrims, in dispensaries, hospitals for the indigent sick, and in the humane treatment of animals and men—had a profound influence on Chinese life.

Confucianism, Taoism and Buddhism did not entirely overlap, but a man of T'ang could, in a single day, pay his respects to the deified heroes of the past, attend a pious Buddhist pageant showing a jewelled lord saving humble souls from the pains of hell, and practice the gymnastics and breathing exercises prescribed by the Taoists to prepare for ultimate transfiguration. Each supplied a different answer to man's most searching questions.

If a man asked, "What must I do among other men in this everyday world?" Confucianism supplied the answer: "Rely on the wisdom of the ancient sages, correctly interpreted". The role of the Confucian gentleman was that of the responsible citizen, aware of his duties to his civilization and of his relationship to the eternal powers that both threatened and preserved him. This relationship was dramatized by the State religion and elucidated by the Confucian arts of philology and history.

If a man asked, "What is my place in nature?" Taoism supplied the answer: "You are part of it, and must understand its subtle ways—to your own advantage". From this understanding came technology and natural science, a sense of the relativity of human values in the great scheme of things, an awareness of the idleness of ambition, and a vision of eternity anticipated in wild places, in gardens, in painting and in poetry.

If a man asked, "What can I hope for beyond this world?" Buddhism supplied the answer: "Search the holy scriptures for the truth about the illusions of appearances and the goadings of your passions". It was possible to understand the very nature of existence itself, and to base a morality on that understanding; a Buddhist could contemplate the character of the mind and the possibility of real knowledge and find faith and hope beyond transient human codification.

A THOUSAND BUDDHAS, *or "Enlightened Ones", in a mountain-side gallery at Mai-chi-shan in northern China, embody the message that all men can be saved.*

BUDDHISM IN STONE

During the first century B.C., Indian missionaries in China began to preach the revolutionary word of the Buddha, the "Enlightened One" who had lived in India some 500 years earlier. Buddhism taught doctrines new to the Chinese: that existence is suffering, that the individual is repeatedly reborn to lead many lives and that the soul can escape into eternal peace by extinguishing the self. Unlike the social code of Confucianism or the more primitive nature worship of Taoism, the new religion charted a route to a world beyond the grave.

For a time the alien faith was a powerful force that shaped China's thought and art. In the centuries of political turmoil that followed the collapse of the Han dynasty in A.D. 220, many disillusioned intellectuals embraced the doctrines of Buddhism and millions of peasants found solace in its other-worldliness. After the tenth century, the tide of Buddhism receded before a renascent Confucianism; but it left behind at various sites in the mountains of its adopted land some of the world's most moving sculpture, monuments to the contemplative spirit of man.

GRAVEN GUARDIANS OF THE FAITH

The custom of erecting Buddhist images in caves began in India and was brought by missionaries across Asian trade routes into China. In this new land, the doctrine and rich iconography of Buddhism satisfied a deep spiritual hunger. Rulers and wealthy families, hoping to earn merit for the afterlife, financed the carving of thousands of devotional images out of solid rock.

But Buddhism and its art were inevitably altered by their encounter with Chinese culture. Under the influence of Taoism and local Chinese folk-religions, figures were added to the original Buddhist pantheon. Some of these figures were gentle and meditative. Others, like the Heavenly Guardian against evil shown on the right, displayed a ferocity that bore little resemblance to the ascetic, quietly contemplative nature of Indian Buddhism.

AT THE ENTRANCE OF A CAVE *stand two minor figures of Buddhist sculpture—a maidenly attendant (left) and a King of Heaven who protected the Buddha from evil spirits (right).*

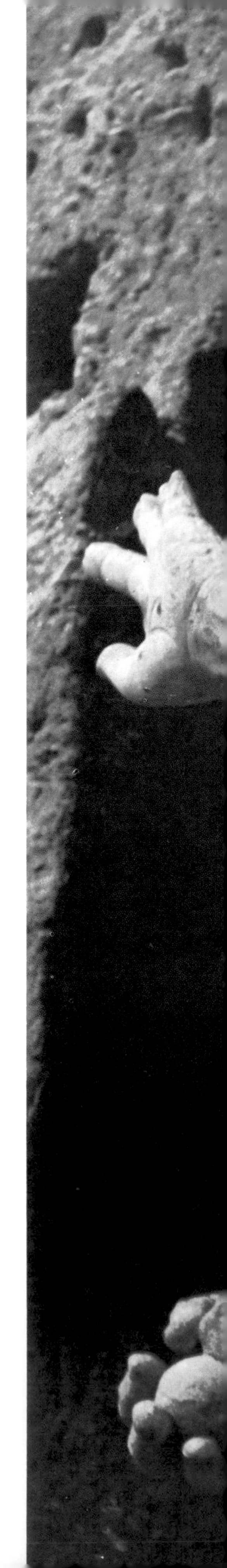

SERENE FOLLOWERS OF THE BUDDHA

Repose, inwardness, imperturbability—these were the qualities of a man who accepted the teachings of the Buddha, and from the sixth century onwards Chinese sculptors were masters at revealing such characteristics in stone. The human aspect of Buddhism was eloquently expressed in statues of the so-called *lohans*, who were actual apostles, disciples or missionaries of the Buddha. A *lohan* was a man who had comprehended the essential meaning of the Buddha's words—that an escape from the suffering of existence was possible only if worldly passions were completely extinguished. Buddhist devotions involved constant meditation on this theme. And worshippers at the shrines were deeply moved by the sight of prayerful disciples carved in rock—not gods, but men like themselves, who had achieved the calm detachment that was Buddhism's goal.

DISCIPLES OF THE BUDDHA *often appeared in Chinese sculpture. On the right is Kasyapa, a Hindu monk converted by the Buddha. The lohan opposite is thought to be Ananda, the youngest disciple.*

THE COMPASSIONATE BODHISATTVAS

As practised in India, early Buddhism preached that every man must strive alone to escape into eternal peace from a cycle of reincarnation. The version of Buddhism that became popular in China was different. It elaborated on the concept of bodhisattvas—godlike beings, sometimes called "potential Buddhas", who postponed their own salvation so that they could help living men to find the true path. Various bodhisattvas were endowed with the power to dispel greed, to protect men against ghosts who might interfere with spiritual practices and to confer merit on the faithful. The worship of these compassionate spirits could fulfil even such worldly desires as financial success and a family of many children. So flexible was the concept that one sixth-century emperor won the title of "Saviour Bodhisattva" by his generous gifts to Buddhist temples.

A BODHISATTVA *is portrayed in the typical stone statue as a figure with elaborately coiffed hair. Carved around* A.D. *490, this example is at Yün-kang, well-known site of the earliest cave sculpture in China.*

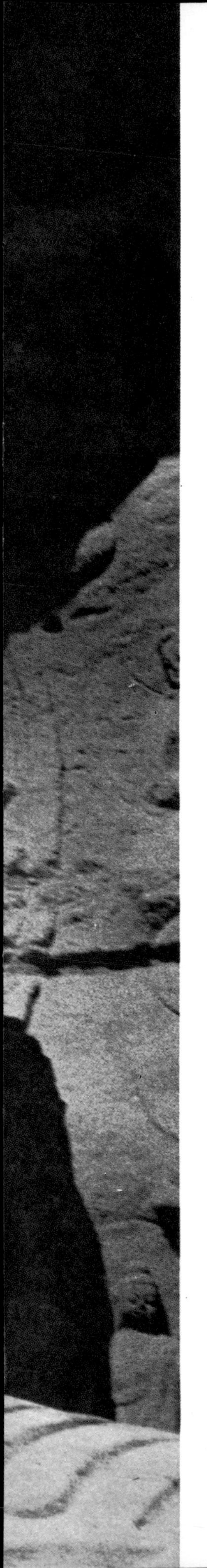

THE MANY BUDDHAS OF CHINA

Huge figures of Buddhas dominated cave shrines in China—not necessarily *the* Buddha, for the Chinese worshipped many divine Buddhas, as well as the godlike bodhisattvas. The historical Buddha (*left*), who lived in India around 500 B.C., was regarded as a spiritual leader, to be emulated rather than worshipped. But the most popular Chinese form of the faith emphasized other Buddhas —literally millions of them, by some reckonings— who dwelt in eternity as gods and had never been men. During the T'ang Dynasty—the height of the Buddhist age of China—most Chinese worshipped the Buddha Amitabha, Lord of the Western Paradise. It was popularly believed that a sincere utterance of Amitabha's name guaranteed a worshipper rebirth into this paradise, a radiant land made of lapis lazuli and dotted with jewelled trees.

AN ALL-KNOWING COLOSSUS, *a statue of the historical Buddha gazes from a cliff at Yün-kang. The head alone is 13 feet high.*

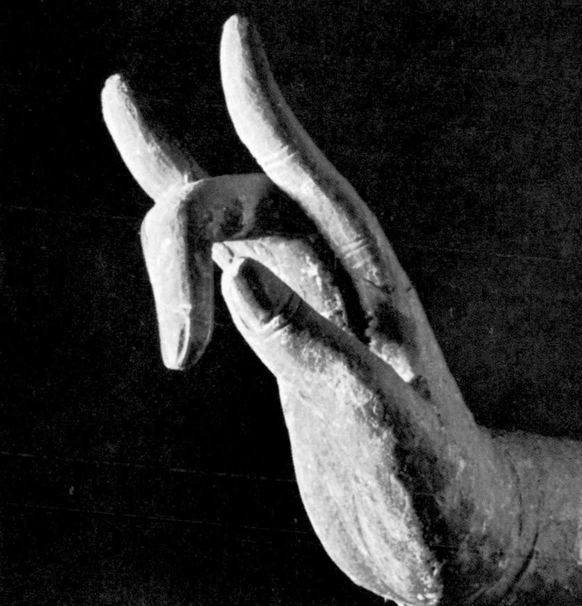

SPIRITUAL SYMBOLS (*right*) *are present in the statues of all Buddhas. The head knot indicates that the Buddha is all-wise. The hand position indicates that he is conversing. The "lotus" position of the feet, turned towards heaven, means he is meditating.*

A GALLERY OF DIVINE FIGURES *at Lung-men in central China displays a 50-foot-high Buddha flanked by a bodhisattva (centre) and two guardians (right).*

Carved in the seventh century, the Lung-men Buddha is Vairocana, then believed to be the one Buddha who had created the universe and all other Buddhas.

4

ROYAL SONS OF HEAVEN

THE LEGENDARY EMPEROR YÜ *was reputed to have founded the dynastic system as the first ruler of the Hsia Dynasty in the 23rd century* B.C. *The Great Yü, as he was known, is credited with having built new waterways and a drainage system that controlled the flood-ridden Yellow river valley.*

The monarchs of Ancient China received their mandate to rule from Heaven. They were men, but they were divine men, and they mediated between their spiritual parent Heaven and the actual world called "Under-Heaven".

This idea that a great power in the sky conferred upon one especially worthy superman and his successors the right to rule all men goes back to the prehistoric mists that conceal the beginnings of Chinese history. From ancient legends of awesome nature-gods, oral tradition handed down tales of the first kings of all, the true "Sons of Heaven". They were the ultimate patriarchs, the founders of the Chinese nations of the past. In the fragments of ancient literature that remain they appear as the offspring of the union of earthly mothers with the heavenly deity, whose power showed itself in the thunder, whose majesty was represented by the sun and whose grace revealed itself in the fertilizing rain.

Direct descent from the sky-god, the great source of fertility on high, was the basis of all claims to royal legitimacy. The early "Sons of Heaven" were believed to be endowed with extraordinary spiritual power, obtained directly from their heavenly parent. This enabled them to establish hereditary dynasties of holy kings, but the precious spiritual power was not passed on intact to successive generations. Gradually it dissipated itself until finally a king who was completely devoid of it inherited the throne. Heaven then withdrew its mandate from him and bestowed it anew on a hero of a different lineage.

The story of the evolution of the concept of kingship might be said to begin with Yao, one of the most ancient of the legendary rulers of primeval times. In tribal myth, he was a personified mountain who towered over his watery domain for countless years: "Yao's frame, approached closely, was like the sun; seen from afar, it was like a cloud". Later, he was represented as a noble though extraordinary monarch who ruled during prehistoric times.

Yao's most famous successors were Shun, who originally, it seems, was the master of the elephants that lurked in the dark forests, and Yü the Great, who made dry land available for the dwelling places

A JADE PI *(pronounced "bee")—a flat disc with a round hole symbolizing Heaven—was used in ceremonies by early Chinese kings when they appealed to celestial spirits. Such objects were also often placed in royal graves.*

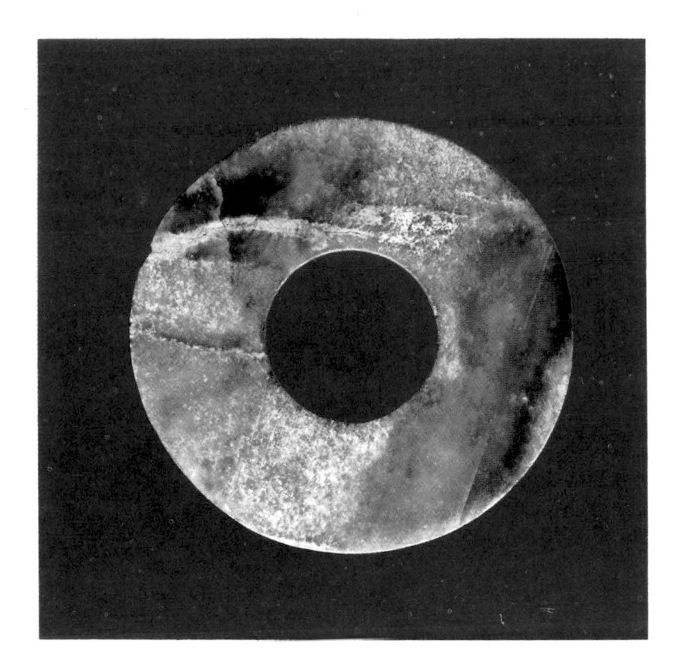

of mortal men in the midst of the primeval waters:

> *When widespread waters swelled to Heaven and serpents and dragons did harm, Yao sent Yü to control the waters and to drive out the serpents and dragons. The waters were controlled and flowed to the east. The serpents and dragons plunged to their places.*

On this land Yü the Great is believed to have established the Hsia kingdom, a society that may actually have existed around 2000 B.C. but for which there is no archaeological or historical evidence. In the official accounts, Yü is described as a true "Son of Heaven", born of a virgin who ate seeds, known to us as "Job's Tears", that contained the divine sperm of the sky-god. He is said to have passed the throne on to his son, thereby establishing the first hereditary dynasty of true men.

Over the centuries, traditional belief was to become indistinguishable from historical fact, and the naïve tales of the first "Sons of Heaven" were to lead to the concept of the dazzling, sacrosanct ruler of medieval China. One dynasty after another was to receive the mandate from Heaven and rule China until its spiritual power had been spent—a decline that often existed only in the political propaganda of the successful revolutionaries who founded succeeding dynasties.

The semi-legendary Hsia Dynasty founded by Yü the Great is said to have been overthrown by the Bronze Age King T'ang, traditionally the first historical ruler of China, who, according to accepted tradition, was born of a mother made pregnant by a bird's egg that fell from Heaven. He was the first king of the Shang Dynasty, which ruled the Middle Kingdom from about 1500 B.C. until about 1000 B.C.

The most important function of the Bronze Age king was to communicate with the spirit world—the gods of nature who were the source of his power and provided life-giving rain, and the ghosts of his departed ancestors whose infinite wisdom guided his actions. He did this in a number of ways.

From fragmentary literature of later times it appears that the ancient kings were believed to be able to renew their heaven-derived power from liaisons with rain-goddesses—lovely nymphs, clothed in swirling mists, who haunted sacred mounds and mountains, cloudy peaks and healing springs. Chinese myths that preserve faded remembrances of early religion abound with references to the ritual matings of these goddesses with the king in the role of shaman—the medium between man and the spirit world. In such rituals the king became the temporary embodiment of Heaven and sought the love of a divine woman who could hardly be distinguished from the ancestress of his own clan. Indeed, the authority of the earliest Chinese kings appears to have derived as much from their intimacy with lovely female rain-spirits as from their kinship to revered kings of the past.

The archaic kings also got in touch with the gods of nature to make sure that Heaven provided adequate water for the dusty farmlands of the Middle Kingdom. In times of drought, it was the duty of the king to perform sacrifices to the gods, using elaborate bronze ritual vessels; it was also his function as the chief shaman to communicate directly with the sources of rain, high and low, whether in the form of a dragon, a rainbow-goddess or even the sky-god himself. He could also seek the help of rain-gods by staging a ritual dance in which the demon causing the drought was sacrificed. The king himself might participate in this ritual and dance under the hot sky, finally stripping off his robes and exposing his nude body to symbolic destruction by the blistering rays of the sun. In cases of extreme drought, a performer acted as proxy for the king, and, after completing the ritual dance, was indeed burned to death in a ceremony in which the earthly fire represented the solar fire in the sky. This important rite, modified with the rise of civilized sensibilities to omit human sacrifice and other barbarisms, continued to be performed down into medieval times. The shamanistic role of the "Son of Heaven" as intermediary between gods and men was never quite forgotten.

These communications with heavenly deities were equalled in importance by the exchanges between the kings of Shang and the ghosts of the venerable King T'ang and other royal ancestors. The records of some of these messages form one of the most significant archaeological discoveries of our century—the now-famous "oracle bones".

Just north of the Yellow river, in the classical heartland of China, lies the town of Anyang. Here, at the site of a great city of the Bronze Age, were found many inscribed tortoise-shells and animal bones. First sold casually as prehistoric dragon bones, these relics were later discovered to contain the record of messages between the living and dead kings of Shang.

When the king wished to consult the divine will or foresight of one of these exalted spirits he had the royal diviner scratch his message on a flat, polished piece of bone. The diviner then applied a red-hot bar to a hole drilled in the bone and the intense heat produced a pattern of cracks. From this pattern the diviner interpreted the reply sent to the king by his long-dead ancestors. One worried question has been translated as "Will there be any calamities within the next ten days?" How the diviner deciphered the spirit's reply is unknown—the answers were hidden in a pattern of cracks that the diviner usually had to take as meaning "yes", "no" or "undecided".

Faithful communication with ancestors was more important for kings than for ordinary people—their ancestors were more powerful and could have greater influence on the welfare of the whole nation. These ghostly forefathers were, in a real sense, the true rulers of Ancient China. To living men they represented the great unbroken stream of life, extending back to the hallowed past. They watched over the ritual springtime matings on river banks: they brought the seasonable rains that set the green shoots of millet springing in the fields of the farmers; they told the ancient kings and chieftains the best days for huntings, for sacrificing, for planting and for any of the thousand ritualized activities that made up the lives of these masters of mankind.

Around 1000 B.C. the Shang Dynasty collapsed. The last Shang ruler, the official story of later times said, was a man of great personal strength and eloquence, but he had allowed his Court to become so corrupt that it engaged in indecent, naked revels. Such decadence was an indication that the spiritual power of the line had been used up, and finally the king, abandoned by Heaven, burned himself in his spendid palace.

Heaven transferred its mandate to the house of Chou, the militant rulers of a small province to the west who swept across the Middle Kingdom and ruthlessly destroyed the Shang capital. The new dynasty was to rule China until the third century B.C.

The men of Chou had their own revered mother, distinct from the deified mother of the Shang.

According to legend, she had stepped into the footprint of a huge, divine being and bore the totemic ancestor of the Chou line of kings. Later tradition was to transform a descendant of this union, Wen Wang, from a petty chieftain whose son led the conquest of Shang into a wise suzerain endowed with superhuman moral and political talents:

Wen Wang is placed above—
how radiant in Heaven!
Although Chou is an old domain,
its Mandate is a new one.
The holders of Chou—
were they not brilliant?
The Mandate of god—
is it not timely?
Wen Wang ascends, descends,
to the left and right of god.

Gradually, said the official story, the kings of Chou also became corrupt and decadent. A legend illustrating their supposed irresponsibility tells of one King Yu who almost caused the overthrow of the dynasty in the eighth century B.C. by indulging the whims of a beautiful but capricious and unsmiling concubine with whom he was infatuated. Finally the king thought of a way to make her laugh. He ordered the city's beacon fires to be lit—a signal to the feudal lords that they should rush to the capital with their armies to resist barbarian invasion. When the fierce barons and their troops converged on the palace at full gallop, brandishing their swords, and found nobody to fight, they looked so ridiculous to the lady that she laughed merrily. Soon afterwards a real invasion took place and the flares were lit. This time no help came and the city fell.

The dynasty survived but the secular power of the kings continued to decline. The gradual weakening of the kings, after some three centuries of rule, appeared to coincide with the rising power of the feudal lords. Barons who controlled large fiefs seized and retained all political and military power, ignoring the ineffectual king, who sat in his capital surrounded by his ministers and policy makers, a host of minor administrators, judges, diviners, bath supervisors, dyers, lapidaries, bronze-smiths and many others. These shadowy kings appear in the fragmentary and biased documents only as aloof puppets, the tools of self-seeking lords.

Only the priestly functions remained the prerogative of the "Son of Heaven". Just how many of the archaic duties of the shaman-king were still performed by the Chou kings of the fifth century B.C. is not revealed by contemporary texts. It is clear, however, that the monarchs of declining Chou, whether or not they continued the ritual soul-matings with rain-goddesses and the like, did inherit many of the complex requirements and taboos appropriate to a ceremonial and magical king. The orientation of their halls, the designs and colours of their costumes, the ingredients of their meals, all were strictly regulated according to the season of the year, so that their every act would correspond to the momentary condition of their eternal relationship with the forces generated in Heaven. The correct observance of all seasonable rites ensured the maintenance of the natural order, an abundance of crops and the health of the people. But by this time the rituals had deteriorated into highly formalized—but almost perfunctory—ceremony.

It was into this world of narrow royal authority and widespread political anarchy that the itinerant sage Confucius brought his vision of the resurrection of a glorious past. He and his followers re-emphasized the purely divine origin of royal duties and powers. An eminent Confucianist of the fourth century B.C., known to us as Mencius, explained the king's heritage in a dialogue concerning the transfer of rule from Yao to Shun:

Wang Chang said, "Is it the case that Yao gave all Under-Heaven to Shun?"
Mencius said, "Not so—the Son of Heaven has not the power to give all Under-Heaven to any man".
Wang Chang said, "So it may be—still, Shun surely possessed all Under-Heaven. Who gave it to him?"
Mencius said, "Heaven gave it to him!"

Faithful and honourable use of these divinely granted powers was the king's most important duty in the Confucianists' view. They held up as examples to be emulated those ancient Utopias that had been presided over by such Heaven-blessed kings as Yao, Shun and Yü the Great. These benign kings of antiquity, the Confucianists said, had shown their concern for the welfare of their subjects by bestowing on them the arts of civilization. A similar social responsibility was thus required of kings of any time: kings must be all powerful, but they must also care for the physical welfare of the lands and peoples entrusted to them.

The society that ultimately emerged out of the ruins of Chou feudalism was essentially Confucian in its insistence upon a Utopian ideology and a rigid social hierarchy; it was theocratic, aristocratic and bureaucratic. One tendency of Confucian thought later régimes would find highly useful; the Confucianists emphasized paternal care on the part of divinely ordained autocrats, and willing obedience on the part of an orderly populace. This philosophy would prove an invaluable justification for the imperialist-minded monarchs of Han and later dynasties.

Yet after the fall of the Chou Dynasty in the third century B.C. it seemed for a time that the ideals of Confucius might be forgotten. Ying Cheng, ruler of the militant State of Ch'in, eliminating other claimants to the trembling throne of Chou, brought the whole of China under one rule, as Confucius had envisaged, but he did not adhere to the teachings of that sage.

The ministers of Ch'in were followers of a school of political doctrine that had gained prominence during the brutal years of the fourth century B.C., the school of Legalists. They thought that government could become a science only if governors were not deceived by such pious, unworkable abstractions as "humanity" and "tradition". In the view of this group, attempts to improve the human situation by ethical precepts and noble example were bound to be useless. What was needed was strong government and a carefully devised code of law, stringently and impartially enforced. Wang Ch'ung, the first-century A.D. philosopher, summed up the attitude of the Legalists in this fashion:

Make standards clear
Give precedence to achievement.
If the 'good' are not profitable to the nation do not supply rewards.
If the 'unworthy' are not harmful to good order, do not apply penalties.

For a while it seemed that these hard-headed, utilitarian doctrines might triumph. Indeed, the founder of Ch'in hoped that his totalitarian government would endure for ever.

He disdained the old title *wang*, "king", which had long been devalued by its repeated usurpation by other great lords in the last years of Chou. In its place he created for himself the title *huang ti*, often translated as "emperor", which would remain the highest title of the rulers of China until 1911. The first word, *huang*, connoted "radiant, illustrious, glorious", and was used in ancient times to describe celestial divinities. The second word, *ti*, was the title of the highest spirit-kings of Shang.

The Ch'in founder also usurped the old title of "Son of Heaven", until then the prerogative of the kings of Chou in direct line of descent from T'ien, "Heaven". He became a divine monarch modelled after the old holy kings of Shang and Chou. He bore a strong resemblance to the deified Greek kings of Egypt and Syria or to the Roman Caesars—the "Divine Augusti"—with their own temples and priesthoods.

The mighty Ch'in empire barely survived the lifetime of its brilliant founder; it was overthrown by civil war three years after his death. Probably the most important factor contributing to his overthrow was the unquenchable resentment of the feudal barons against encroachment on their powers. Another was undoubtedly the deep-rooted loyalty of the populace to the traditions associated with the holy kings of their forefathers.

After several years of anarchy a military officer named Liu Pang, a man of peasant stock, succeeded in uniting the Middle Kingdom under the Han Dynasty in the year 202 B.C. This less centralized empire was to succeed where Ch'in had failed; it was to become the Roman Empire of the East.

Fundamental to its success was the establishment of a State religion, the sole purpose of which was to maintain the power, majesty and divine authority of the monarch and the cosmic system he represented. Based on surviving fragments of late Chou books associated with Confucius and his followers, this religion held that the ruler was responsible for the well-being of his people and for setting an example of moral virtue.

One ideal formulation of the role of the Han Son of Heaven was drawn up by Tung Chung-shu, a theorist who believed in rigid mathematical proportion in social arrangements and therefore divided the emperor's responsibilities into three parts.

He makes the sacrifice (to Heaven) in the suburb with utmost respect;
He serves his forefathers in the ancestral shrines;
He elevates and illuminates both filial and fraternal piety;
He displays what is unique in filial conduct.
By these means he honours the Heavenly base.

He holds the ritual plough and tills in person;
He gathers the mulberry and tends the silk worms himself;
He breaks the grassland and propagates cereals;
He opens ground and clears it away—for adequate clothing and food.
By these means he honours the Earthly base.

He founds a Round Academy and village centres of learning;
He cultivates filial and fraternal piety, respect and deference;
He enlightens through instruction and conversion;
He inspires by ceremony and music.
By these means he honours the Human base.

The secular administration of the realm from Han times on was delegated to a vast bureaucracy comprising great ministers of State, private officers of the semi-divine household of the emperor, military mandarins and their elegant guard divisions, as well as the less-glamorous bureau chiefs, tax experts, censors, inspectors, civil engineers and agents of State monopolies. All these were responsible to the chief ministers who were, in turn, directly responsible to the "Son of Heaven" for the proper conduct of the nation's affairs. Chief ministers were usually appointed in pairs as Ministers of the Left and Right, each checking and balancing the other. Some were members of old and powerful families; some were political geniuses risen from the ranks. Their rise might be spectacular and their power and wealth immense—but their ruin could be swift and total.

Although the emperor's hold over the populace through the State religion and the bureaucracy was very strong, the sovereigns of Han were still conscious of their irregular inheritance of the sacred throne of Chou. They therefore justified the seizure of power by the founder of their dynasty by formalizing and exploiting the old belief that the Mandate of Heaven could expire. As promulgated in Han times, this theory provided legitimacy to successful revolutionists and permitted the founding of new dynasties by those not descended from the sky-god and an earthly mother. This doctrine held that Heaven could hand down its mandate to any virtuous hero, imbuing him with spiritual force so potent that all mankind must submit to him; Heaven could also withdraw its mandate from an unworthy ruler. The virtuous sword of a new "Son of Heaven" could then bring the corrupt dynasty to an ignominious end.

This flexible doctrine of kingship legitimized Han claims to the heavenly mandate, but it also made the dynasty vulnerable to pretenders and adventurers. Well aware that their power and glory were not guaranteed for ever, these new "Sons of Heaven" surrounded themselves with magicians, shamans and diviners whose duty it was to watch earth and sky for signs of Heaven's judgement on their reigns—indications of the prospects of their continued tenure.

Heavenly tokens might appear at any time or place—in a remote province or at the gates of the palace itself. For example, ancient swords found rotting in the soil were crucial omens. They were regarded as weapons of power left by Heaven for the use of a future hero who would receive the mandate to rule. Rust and patina merely disguised the hidden spiritual power, which might flash forth as a purple glow. It was the duty of the corps of diviners to interpret such omens for the king so that he could take action to forestall revolution.

Favourable omens—the appearance of a white peacock, the vision of a dragon in the aurora borealis or the unearthing of a mysteriously inscribed jade —were widely publicized. Upon receipt of the pleasing report, a delegation was dispatched to the scene to authenticate the lucky find. If it was an immovable object, such as a holy tree, an artist went along to delineate the form. When the omen had been duly documented, Court poets were required to compose intricately worded odes in its praise.

The occasion was celebrated all over the empire with the proclamation of feast days, amnesties for convicts and often the formal declaration of a new era—perhaps named "Red Crow' or something equally appropriate, such as "Yellow Dragon" or "Eternal Harmony"—slogans as meaningful and hopeful in Chinese antiquity as the era names proclaimed by contemporary leaders—"New Deal", "New Frontier" and "Great Society".

Blessed by the divine message that authorized him to rule over all peoples, the "Son of Heaven" went off to war. Tribute or slavery—these were the choices available to the inferior races destined to be his subjects. The noble joy of mastery over lesser peoples and the pleasures afforded by easy access to domestic slaves and fine gems, furs and perfumes was surely deserved by the agent of Heaven who brought virtue and civilization to all nations. The first-century philosopher Wang Ch'ung wrote of the results of the far-flung conquests of Han:

> *The Jung and Ti tribes of antiquity now participate in the Middle Kingdom; the Naked Men of antiquity are now clothed in Court costume; the bare-headed ones of antiquity are now hatted with blazoned caps, and the barefooted ones of antiquity are now shod with Shang slippers.*

In spite of its power and in spite of its precautions, the Han Dynasty was destined to distintegrate. The States that succeeded it in the north fell into the hands of barbarian invaders who overran

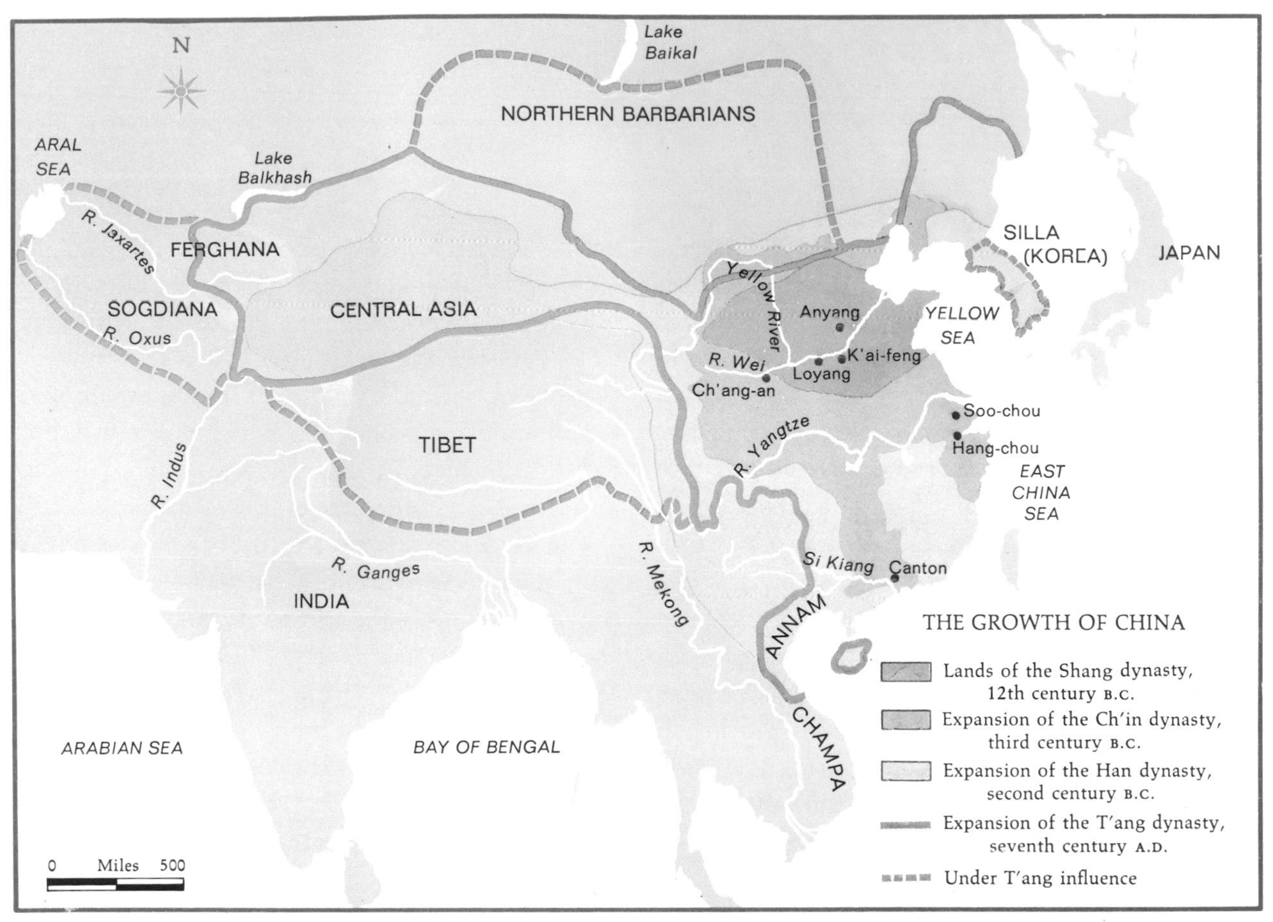

THE EXPANSION OF EMPIRE, *from the small holdings of the Shang dynasty to the giant territory of the T'ang dynasty, is shown above. The first annexations took place during the third and second centuries B.C. But not until some 900 years later did Chinese influence reach its zenith.*

the Middle Kingdom in waves between the third and the sixth centuries A.D. But the great and holy role conceived for the ancient "Son of Heaven" survived even these vicissitudes.

China once again became a great empire in the seventh century under the leadership of the house of T'ang. T'ang armies not only restored all the holdings claimed by earlier dynasties but also extended them to make China the greatest empire in the world. Under the T'ang emperors the unique prestige of the old title "Son of Heaven" was restored, the State religion was revitalized and the vast government bureaucracy once again administered a unified realm. The three centuries of T'ang rule were to be remembered as China's greatest age.

At that time the Chinese monarch became known throughout Asia as a mighty king, comparable only to the Persian King of Kings and the Roman Caesar. His title, "Son of Heaven", became familiar in the medieval West in a variety of translations and paraphrases, all of which attested to his divinity and to the divinity of his imitators. Both *The Thousand and One Nights* and Marco Polo's description of the wonders of the East refer to the King of China as *faghfur*, which is a corruption of an Iranian title meaning "Son of God". The kings of Bactria called themselves Devaputra, "Sons of God", and even the petty kings of medieval Central Asia assumed the title "Son of Heaven", in feeble emulation of the great Chinese original.

The holy atmosphere that enveloped the emperor at great State ceremonies set him apart from ordinary men. These rites included some that would quickly be recognized as part of the State religion, such as the great sacrifice to Heaven in mid-winter, presided over by the emperor, garbed in archaic robes covered with sacred symbols. They also included those ceremonies that we might consider merely political and social, such as the great levees at which the emperor received ambassadors bearing tribute from their humbled sovereigns. On such occasions, the inner Court glittered with gold and figured silks, and the "Son of Heaven" was surrounded by belted archers and halberdiers clad in rich armour and bright capes, bearing regimental ensigns embellished with the shapes of wild horses and leopards. In the form of symbols of submission, the wealth of the Indies and all the East lay piled on the marble floor of the great Palace.

Let us look behind the gorgeous ceremonial robes and the clouds of sandalwood smoke at the brilliant eighth-century Emperor Li Lung-chi, one of the men who inherited the awesome role of the "Son of Heaven". He may be said to epitomize the blend of characteristics typical of his age: worldly sophistication, social responsibility in the Confucian tradition and respect for ancient rites.

Li Lung-chi was a man of strong personality, impressive appearance and exemplary manners. He was as skilled in the manly arts of horsemanship, archery and polo-playing as he was learned in the noble arts of calligraphy, astronomy and music. Indeed, he was an accomplished performer on several musical instruments as well as an informed student of musical theory. He founded academies in his capital for the study of popular music and dancing and kept his own company of actors on the palace grounds. He took a keen interest in scientific and technological problems; among other achievements, his reign is noted for the building of an iron suspension bridge over the Yellow river, its bamboo cables held on the banks by cast-iron supports in the shape of oxen, and for the construction of a water-powered astronomical clock that provided information for a reformed calendar.

Li Lung-chi was also a humane man—he decreed the abolition of the death penalty and founded a hospital for the sick and maimed beggars of the capital city. Twenty years after the beginning of his reign a courtier observed that Li Lung-chi was getting thin. "Let my figure be lean," he replied, "but all under Heaven must be fat."

True to the centuries of tradition that were his heritage, Li Lung-chi exemplified the kingly model described by the followers of Confucius. The T'ang "Son of Heaven" never failed to seek the aid of the mighty but by now almost anonymous deities who radiated energy from the high places of his realm. During the drought of A.D. 723. Li Lung-chi stood on a mat for three days, exposed to the open sky, and prayed for water from Heaven, just as his predecessors, the kings of Shang, had done some 1,700 years before.

But by Li Lung-chi's time the sovereign's role was priestly rather than shamanistic. He could communicate with the spirit world but he was not possessed by the spirit; he merely acted a formal part in an ancient play. However, religious functions were carried out with great strictness, sobriety and attention to detail; the officers in charge of the offerings were flogged if their jade symbols, bolts of precious silk and sacrificial animals were not up to specifications.

Far from the centre of things were the provincial magistrates who were well aware of the importance of their positions yet hopeful that one day they might be called to the glorious capital. They toiled at the essential tasks of collecting taxes and tribute, improving field production and bringing civilized modes of conduct and a sense of confidence in the central government to the ignorant farmers and benighted aborigines in their charge.

Necessarily the actions of these officers were sometimes brutal. A military official, even in the enlightened years of T'ang, occasionally felt obliged to make a pyramid of the heads of perverse rebels or obdurate aborigines as a warning to others who might wish to reject the beneficent rule of the "Son of Heaven". Even a civil official was often required to bring misery and death to the people with whose welfare he was entrusted in order to fulfil the tribute quotas required by the distant Court. Drowned pearl-divers along the southern coast and the broken necks of bird-hunters among the northern crags bear witness to such practices.

The multitude of governors, mayors, petty staff officers and country bureaucrats also had their spiritual duties. They were ex-officio priests of the State religion. Their ordinary religious responsibilities were similar to those of Emperor Li Lung-chi: they were obliged to go through a period of purification before each worship service, fasting, washing their hair, breathing sacred incense and meditating on holy things. The rites over which they presided resembled those held in the great capital—chants, dances, prayers and offerings to the gods.

Such rites were performed at times when there were signs that the spiritual world was out of joint—prolonged drought was a typical occasion. Such a disaster might be blamed on spiritual flaws in the "Son of Heaven" himself, and hence were likely to lead to insurrection and even to the overthrow of the government. Accordingly, the monarch's representatives made sure that every possible avenue of extrication was explored—above all, the good old rituals.

Despite these safeguards, the rich, expansive and creative rule of T'ang was eventually terminated by insurrection, brought about through greed, treachery, ambition and the unavoidable tensions engendered by an expanding empire. An Lu-shan, an illiterate but ambitious barbarian whom Li Lung-chi had befriended and raised to a high army command, precipitated a civil war and brought peace and prosperity to an end. The emperor was compelled to abdicate in 766, though he lived out six more grey years to die at the age of 77.

The T'ang empire continued to exist for another 150 years, though its magnificent imperial domain lay in ruins and its control over internal affairs was constantly weakening.

The beginning of the end is remembered as the 17th March 905, a festival day in the official almanac. On this holiday a great banquet was prepared in the imperial park of Loyang, the ancient capital of the divine kings of Chou, now the eastern capital of T'ang. The host was Chu Ch'üan-chung, all-powerful warlord and protector of his most honoured guest, Emperor Li Tsu, sovereign of the imperial house of T'ang. Pre-eminent among the other silk-clad guests were the nine brothers of the young monarch. Wine was served on the banks of the Pool of Nine Turnings. Then the nine young princes, possible heirs to the throne, were seized by Chu's men, hanged and thrown into the lake.

Two years later, Li Tsu, then 17 years old and surrounded by the creatures of the warlord, submitted a formal instrument of abdication to Chu Ch'üan-chung who had meanwhile eliminated all rival contenders to the throne. Chu Ch'üan-chung then assumed the imperial robes in a city not far from Loyang and declared the inauguration of a new era, hopefully named "Opening of Tranquillity".

On the 25th March 908, the unfortunate Li Tsu, his act on the stage of life done, was discreetly put to death lest he become a rallying point for future revolutions aimed at restoration of the glorious house of T'ang. So ended a tragic and dramatic medieval performance of an archaic drama—the transfer of the mandate of Heaven.

THE IMPERIAL INSTRUCTRESS *pens her "Admonitions" on proper conduct for ladies.*

WOMANLY VIRTUES

Chinese emperors and their courtiers had bevies of wives and concubines, all expected to be models of decorum. Their deportment was not left to chance. The ladies were indoctrinated by an instructress, whose perfectionist rules were recorded in a lofty moral tract entitled *The Admonitions of the Instructress to the Court Ladies.* "Correct your character as with an axe, embellish it as with a chisel", this text commanded in part.

Such expectations were often little more than wishful thinking. The Chinese master who painted the following illustrations for the tract recognized that ladies preferred gossip, primping and intrigues to moral improvement. His pictures are tinged with an irony as delicate as the strokes of his sensitive brush.

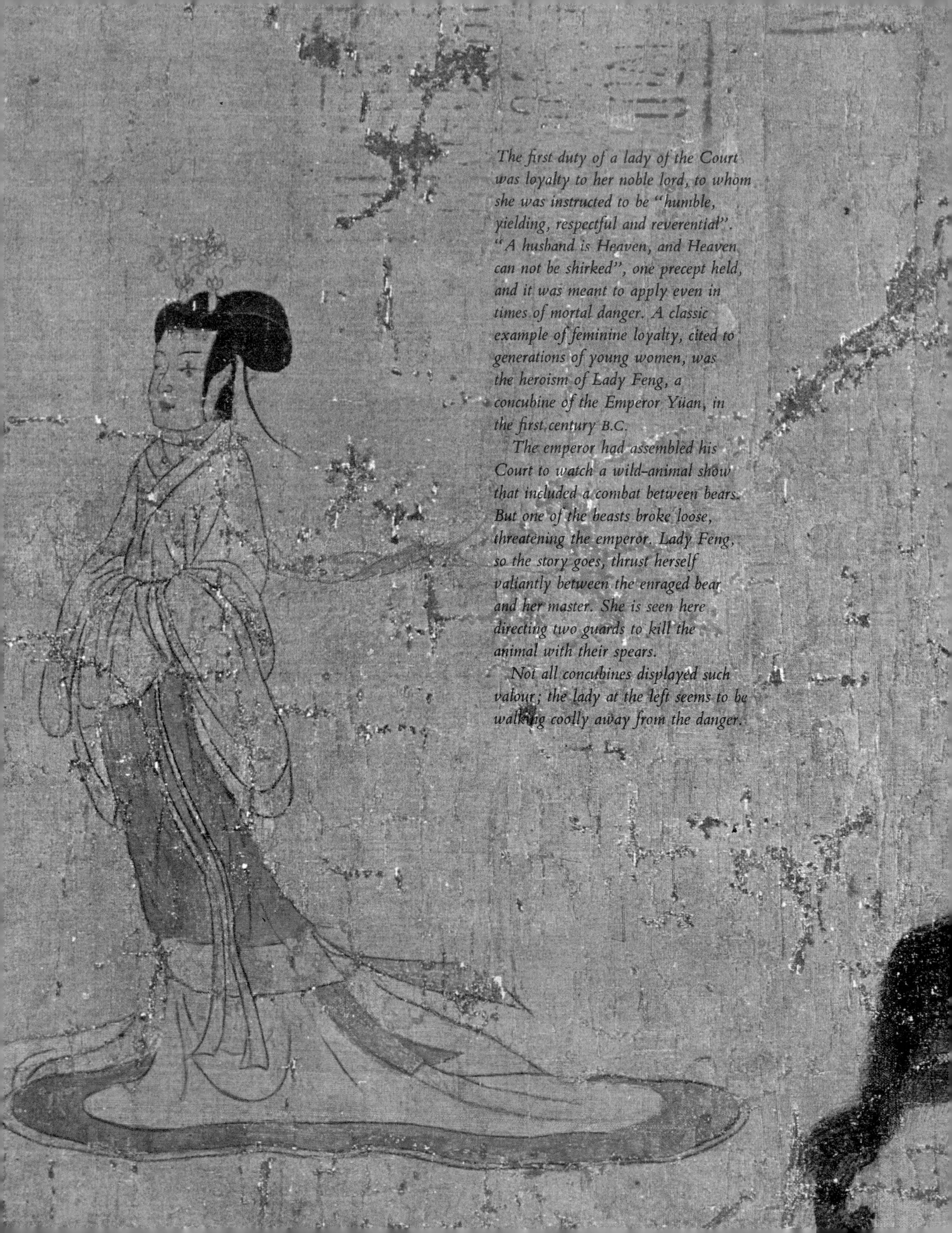

The first duty of a lady of the Court was loyalty to her noble lord, to whom she was instructed to be "humble, yielding, respectful and reverential". "A husband is Heaven, and Heaven can not be shirked", one precept held, and it was meant to apply even in times of mortal danger. A classic example of feminine loyalty, cited to generations of young women, was the heroism of Lady Feng, a concubine of the Emperor Yüan, in the first century B.C.

The emperor had assembled his Court to watch a wild-animal show that included a combat between bears. But one of the beasts broke loose, threatening the emperor. Lady Feng, so the story goes, thrust herself valiantly between the enraged bear and her master. She is seen here directing two guards to kill the animal with their spears.

Not all concubines displayed such valour; the lady at the left seems to be walking coolly away from the danger.

The humble routines of family life were also regulated by the rigid code of courtly manners. A dutiful woman never addressed her lord by name, and handed him objects on a tray, lest she breach propriety by inadvertently touching his hand. Children could visit their father only once every 10 days and then they were enjoined never to "sit down, stand on one foot, lean against an object . . . spit or blow their noses" in his presence.

But these unrealistic restrictions were largely ignored even among the most exalted aristocracy; as this touching domestic scene suggests. The noble father (far right) watches benignly as a woman arranges the hair of a protesting son (centre), while another lady attempts to distract the child with a toy. In the background, a young man reads a scroll to a younger boy and girl.

勿謂幽昧神聽無響無矜尒榮天道惡

盈無恃尒貴隆〻者墜〻鑒于小星戒彼攸

遂比心螽斯則繁尒類

微榮辱由茲勿謂玄漠靈鑒無象

In the privacy of the imperial bedchamber women were allowed more freedom than elsewhere. Even so, they were admonished to avoid frivolity and idle talk. "If the words you utter are good," wrote the instructress, "men . . . will make response to you. But if you depart from this principle, even your bedfellow will distrust you."

In this scene the lady apparently did not heed the instructress's advice, as her bedfellow gives her a quizzical—if not "distrustful"—look while gingerly removing his slippers.

The great concern lavished on the deportment of the Court ladies was counterbalanced by almost total disregard for their intellectual development. Few imperial concubines were taught to read, write or enjoy other pleasures of the mind. They frittered away their time on their persons—arranging their hair (left) or painting their eyebrows (right) in the styles of the day, which bore such exotic names as "Distant Mountains" or "Sorrow Brows". The instructress complained that women knew how to adorn their faces, but not their souls.

人咸知脩其容莫知飾其性之
不飾或愆禮正斧之藻之克念作
聖

Almost from birth Chinese women were taught to be subservient. In olden times girl babies were cradled on the floor to symbolize their inferiority; this, it was hoped, would help to shape a paragon of virtuous docility, like the exquisite creature shown here. Seated humbly, with hands in sleeves, she seems to personify the instructress's final admonition: "Fulfil your duties calmly and respectfully; reflect before you act. This shall win you honour and glory".

Indeed, throughout Chinese history gentle manners helped women to gain personal favours and even worldly power. In the second century B.C. Emperor Liu Ch'e was so enchanted by the demeanour of a slave girl that he installed her in his palace as his empress. Her brother was made a general, her nephew an important political adviser, and eventually her family came to control the empire.

5
A COSMIC PLAN

FILIAL PIETY *is extolled in the story of Tung Yung, who sold himself into bondage to get the money to bury his father. Two scenes on a sixth-century sarcophagus show him toiling in the field (left), and meeting a beautiful maiden (right) who was sent from Heaven to free him from his servitude.*

Whatever roles in life they played or whatever gods they worshipped, the men of Ancient China viewed themselves as actors performing on a cosmic stage. They were primarily concerned with the structure and form of the world in which they lived and with the mysterious forces that operated within the geometric framework of that world.

This framework consisted of the flat platform of earth, permeated by subterranean pipelines carrying vitalizing fluids, and surmounted by the canopy of Heaven studded with the fiery stars that controlled human destiny. The whole scene was believed to be invisibly criss-crossed by lines of force and surging power.

All men accepted the fact that this great picture of the universe could be reduced to a symbolic pattern or miniature replica and incorporated into the design of a holy shrine, the structure of a palace, the plan of a city and the layout of a garden. In each of these the men of Ancient China could trace with some exactitude the patterns of the natural order that directed the actors on the cosmic stage—the guide-lines to the location of the entrances and props and to the paths that must be taken to follow them wisely. Whether Buddhist or Taoist, Confucianist or unbeliever, all studied the secret geometry of the universe, tried to comprehend it, to sketch it, and to imitate it in man-made structures.

The physical universe—the earth and sky—was visualized as a unit. According to the old imagery, sky and earth together made up the parts of a great chariot, its flat carriage-bed shaded by an umbrella on a slightly tilted pole. "Canopy Heaven" was a blue dome covering "Chassis Earth", the yellow flatlands.

The origin of this physical world does not seem to have concerned the men of Ancient China very much, despite their great interest in its shape. A few creation myths survive, but creator-spirits did not figure significantly in their religion—a striking difference from Judaism and Christianity. It appears that the stories of the creator-gods known to the men of the Bronze Age had been almost entirely forgotten when the classical books were coded under the Han emperors, yet one of them was still remembered. This concerned the goddess

Nü Kua, the builder of the sky. The first-century-A.D. critic Wang Ch'ung recorded what he knew of her ancient myth:

> *Nü Kua smelted and refined five-coloured stones with which to repair the blue sky. She cut off the legs of a giant sea-turtle to stand as four sky-poles. But since the sky is deficient in the north-west, the sun and moon move through it there; and since it is deficient in the south-east, the hundred rivers pour through it there.*

After Han times, Nü Kua faded away to become a mere fairy-tale being, neglected by the upper classes and ignored in the State religion. For most men the world was simply *there*, as had been ordained by Heaven since eternity.

The yellow earth itself was neatly subdivided into nine regions, each with its own special characteristics. These were first thought of as the land immediately surrounding the Middle Kingdom—the old central plain—but as knowledge of distant places increased, the boundaries were pushed back farther and farther.

The origin of the concept of the Nine Lands goes back to Yü the Great, conqueror of man-hating water creatures and founder of the semi-legendary Hsia dynasty. Yü is said to have drained the nine regions to provide land for man to live on and to have laid out the courses of the waterways, the original rivers of the world, that separated them. In the ideal, geometric scheme of things, so dear to the old Chinese dream of a perfect world, these nine divisions corresponded to the eight cardinal directions, leaving the ninth in the centre for the particular domain of the Son of Heaven.

The mystic meaning of the nine realms is preserved in a classic myth, known to us in a Han-era version. According to the story, a magic diagram of the earth emerged at the command of Heaven from a tributary of the Yellow river, the river Lo, on which was situated the ancient capital of Loyang. This mystical plan, known as the "Lo Document", is believed to have appeared on the carapace of a turtle in the form of a square divided into nine parts *(below)*. Each square had a number and each of the rows of the magic square added up to 15.

4	9	2
3	5	7
8	1	6

In one famous book of the Chou dynasty this diagram was called the "Universal Model" and its nine cells were sometimes called the "Nine Mansions". The terms and the numbers are believed to have been associated with astrology and with the long-lost rituals of the shaman-kings of misty antiquity. Through the magic square, Heaven had graciously allowed mankind a glimpse of one of its ultimate secrets.

The classic picture of the flat, square earth was complicated by the presence of mountains. But these too could be explained: summits came close to Heaven and so could draw readily on heavenly energies. This was particularly true of the mountains believed to have been placed—by divine design—at the four corners of the earth and at its centre. The ancient Chinese thought that they could identify these five sacred mountains among the uplands that surrounded the yellow plain of the Middle Kingdom. They were the cloud-gatherers, the rain-bringers and the snow-accumulating watersheds, the foci of the most important forces that brought fertility to the nation's farmlands. These divine mountains became the sites of religious activities and of permanent religious establishments. The gods were thought to walk on their summits.

Traditionally, the most important of the five was Mount T'ai, the rugged massif that looked down on the west country. To this mountain went the great monarchs of Ancient China with their entire Courts to carry out elaborate ceremonies aimed at renewing their connections with Heaven. In so doing they strengthened their inner powers, lengthened their lives and inaugurated eras of universal peace.

The five mountains completed the Chinese model of the physical universe. Over all was the heavenly umbrella studded with the glittering stars, themselves inhabited by powerful spirits. Below was the ninefold land on which men worked and prayed. Between stood the five sacred mountains that led the divine energies into their proper earthly channels to the benefit of all.

But the energies themselves—bewildering invisible forces of nature—needed to be systematized for easy comprehension. Shortly before the beginning of the Han period in the third century B.C., it seems, simple ways of understanding the forces were being worked out, and during Han times these modes of thought came gradually to prevail among educated men.

The most important of these schemes was a system that postulated two fundamental energies, *yin* and *yang*. The basic meaning of these words were "shaded" (*yin*) and "sunlit" (*yang*). Symbolically, they stood for "female, dark, terrestrial, recessive, cool, submissive", and "male, bright, celestial, aggressive, warm, dominant".

They might be thought of as comparable to negative and positive electricity. The *yin* power reached its climax in the world at the time of the winter solstice. Then the Son of Heaven made the greatest of all sacrifices, the sacrifice to Heaven in the southern suburb of the capital, and brought back the warm celestial force of *yang* to draw the new crops out of the wet soil. The *yang* force reached its own maximum in midsummer and then began to decline, yielding to the power of *yin*.

In the course of time all facets of life—great and small, animate and inanimate—came to be categorized as either *yin*-orientated or *yang*-orientated. The tasty Chinese partridge was considered a *yang* bird because, it was reported, it always took flight towards the south where the solar heat was at a maximum. A typical manifestation of *yin* was the phosphorescence in the sea, which was called "*yin* fire", the cold mysterious fire that welled up from the shadowy depths of the ocean at night. The interplay of *yin* versus *yang* was believed to be present everywhere in the universe and the correct balance between these two forces was thought to be essential to the perfect life.

This simple dualism is represented most prominently in a book, edited in Han times, called the *I Ching*, the "Book of Changes". It is a miscellany of ancient farmers' lore and diviners' prognostics, but it contains an exhaustive list of items that can be associated with either *yin* or *yang*. For example, it defines the *yang* principle as the hot, dry, fertilizing sun-source and goes on to elaborate its meaning in a long chain of associated symbols: "Its image is Heaven, it is suzerain, it is father . . ." and so on, down to jade, ice and horses.

The *I Ching* also purports to be an interpretation of a document on *yin-yang* dualism called the Ho Chart, which was traditionally believed to have been brought to the Ho, or Yellow river, by a dragon horse from Heaven. The chart consists of eight trigrams, or figures of three, made of various combinations of only two symbols that came to be associated with *yin* and *yang*. This set of trigrams and the *I Ching* commentary on them was referred to constantly and used to interpret all kinds of situations. A sage could explain an earthquake or tell a husband how to deal with an errant wife. Even a veterinarian could fit his treatment to the system. There was one remedy for *yang* animals (such as horses, which rise front-end first) and

SYMBOL OF THE NORTH, *the tortoise was one of the five sacred animals of Chinese cosmology. Often, as in this third-century representation, is was shown intertwined with a snake.*

another remedy for *yin* animals (such as camels, which rise hind-end first).

The system quickly took a firm hold in official circles and, although there were severe penalties for daring commoners who presumed to study the most esoteric of these dangerous secrets, it proved to be a boon both to sincere diviners of the future and to all sorts of charlatans. For men who were convinced of the truth of the *yin-yang* idea—and few men seem to have doubted it after Han times—virtually all phenomena could be explained by it.

Important as *yin* and *yang* were to early Chinese thought about the world, these two forces were not the only ones that had to be taken into account. Equally powerful was the set of "Five Activities" named "Water", "Fire", "Wood", "Metal" and "Earth". These, like the *yin-yang* dualism, appear first in books of the fourth and third centuries B.C.

Superficially the "Five Activities" seem to resemble the Four Elements of Western tradition—"Earth", "Air", "Fire" and "Water". But they are not inert "elements" out of which material things are built; they are active dynamic agencies at work in all natural processes.

The Five Activities were associated with the five directions, the five primary colours and the five sacred animals. The four seasons were assigned to four of the Activities, Earth being excluded because it represented all seasons:

To many early Chinese these associations seemed quite natural. It appears appropriate to link Earth with Centre and with Yellow when one considers that the Chinese civilization began on the yellow soil of the valley of the Yellow river, China's second longest, which was believed to be the centre of the world. Similarly, it was not illogical to link the southern part of China with its red soil to the element of fire.

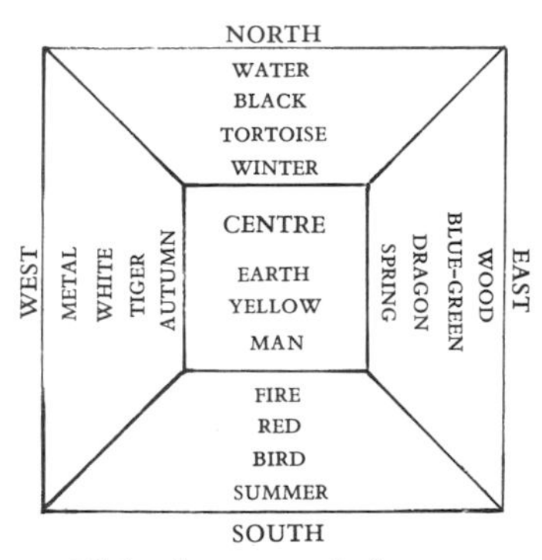

Like *yin* and *yang*, the Activities ultimately acquired an extensive list of additional symbolic correlations, but these were arranged by categories such as tastes, smells, the seasons, domestic animals, sense organs, grains, instruments and even government agencies. Sheep were associated with Wood, fowl with Fire, ox with Earth, dogs with Metal and pigs with Water; the Ministry of Agriculture was linked to Wood, the Ministry of War to Fire, the capital city to Earth, the Ministry of Justice to Metal and the Ministry of Works to Water.

Only one Activity was supposed to be dominant at a given time and each Activity became most important in a fixed sequence. Thus Wood was overcome by Fire, Fire was overcome by Water, and Water was overcome by Earth.

The interworkings of the five, properly understood, accounted for all phenomena and all historical events. Imbalance meant trouble and showed itself in war, plague and famine. The *Book of T'ang* cites the drying up of rivers in the summer of 805 as an example of overactivity of Fire, which caused a derangement in the Water Activity.

Ambitious politicians could promote new dynasties in accordance with the scheme: "Metal" could overcome "Wood"; therefore revolutionaries challenging a dynasty associated with "Wood" were likely to triumph if they carried a white banner since white was associated with "Metal".

In addition to the *yin-yang* and Five Activity theories about cosmic forces, there was an older and less rigid one. In this view, the whole world was criss-crossed by a bewildering variety of vapours or invisible fluids, called *ch'i*. Even the seemingly solid earth was permeated with divine pipelines that carried these vital fluids quickly from one place to another.

Normally their effects were local: those of South China guaranteed the growth of tasty tangerines there; those of North China produced only the thorny lime. But sometimes an unusually powerful focus of force, such as a virtuous, Heaven-approved ruler, could divert a *ch'i* from its normal range. So it was said that the noble Emperor Li Lung-chi drew the *ch'i* from the tropical provinces northwards to his park in Ch'ang-an, causing its tangerines to bear unexpected fruit. When Li Lung-chi was sent into exile, the *ch'i* of the south went awry and the oranges on a holy mountain near Canton failed to appear.

Such was the cosmic geometry of the world and such were the cosmic dynamics that animated it. They could not be ignored and all prudent men studied their hidden secrets. Because it was considered so important for men to conform to the basic patterns in their daily life as well as when performing religious ceremonies, the Chinese tried to model their cities and palaces, their houses and gardens, after the great cosmic patterns. In so doing, they made the perfection of man's Heaven-given environment visible in simplified form.

Special care was taken to consider the natural forces in the construction of sacred buildings, where the shaman-kings of the Bronze Age performed magical and symbolic pantomimes and from which they issued the holy almanac, a divinely inspired calendar for the coming year. The great example of such a building was the sacred hall of the Chou kings, called the "Luminous Hall".

Old books tell us that the design of the Luminous Hall followed the underlying geometry of the universe, but unfortunately no details of the application of this geometry to the actual building have survived. We know only that the "Nine Mansions" of the "Universal Model" of the earth were associated with the magical compartments of this hall. The Luminous Hall remains for us—as it did for the medieval Chinese—a tantalizing vision of antiquity, when men were closer to the gods.

The Luminous Hall vanished before the fall of the Chou Dynasty in the third century B.C., but it was not forgotten. In later eras, when the royal palace had absorbed most of its sacred functions, several attempts were made to restore it as a separate building and institution. But neither the antiquarians nor the ritualists knew its proper form.

The most famous of the reconstructions was carried out in the year 688, during the reign of the Empress Wu, a female "Son of Heaven". She created an elaborate edifice, surmounted by a polished sphere to collect the sacred fires of Heaven, but this must have been very different from the ancient original. The old Luminous Hall had probably been a simple building—a wooden sanctuary where magical aims could be realized even if it did not have fancy marble staircases and iron pillars.

The ancient Luminous Hall is only a single instance of a sacred diagram embodied on a reduced scale in actual wood, earth and stone. In some measure, *all* the royal houses and all the halls of antiquity were similar representations of the cosmic stage, carefully designed for the magical dramas of the Son of Heaven. The rectilinear plan of the world was similarly reflected in the capital cities that appear to have been based in some fashion on the Heaven-given magic square from the river Lo.

Archaeologists have found that the ancient Shang capital excavated at the modern town of Chengchou had an outer wall of rammed earth in the shape of a square, raised on the summit of a Stone Age wall. Probably both the royal capital of Chou and the cities of the great feudal lords were built on the same cosmic plan. Still, we know very little indeed about these Bronze Age cities.

With the establishment of the Han Empire in the third century B.C. the picture becomes much clearer. From that time on there are descriptions of the two great capital cities of the Chinese world: one was Loyang, situated in the north-east on the river Lo; the other was the walled city of Ch'ang-an, "Long Security", on the south bank of the river Wei in a strategic valley traversed by ancient trade routes to Central Asia. The distinguished historian Pan Ku praised the cosmic design of Ch'ang-an and its great palace:

Their frame and image were matched with
Heaven and Earth,
Their warp-lines and weft-lines were
matched with yin and yang.

Other early writers debated the relative glories of the two capitals inconclusively. But the greatest of these writers was a contemporary of Pan Ku, the first-century astronomer Chang Heng, who gave the palm to Ch'ang-an. In his poems he suggested that a capital city properly designed in accordance with cosmic principles would magically compel all the emperor's subject peoples to adopt the Chinese civilization. He therefore praised the wisdom of the founder of the Han Dynasty in his selection of the right position for his capital:

For his purpose, he took thought of the
spirits of Heaven and Earth,
That he might suitably determine the place
that was to be the Heavenly City.

Chang Heng's eulogies also praised the buildings and public places of the capital—the jewelled palace of the Han Emperor Liu Ch'e, built on its quintuple terrace of rammed earth and painted with representations of Heaven, Earth and all the gods; the teeming market-places; and the vast parks, abounding in every sort of fish and game.

The great metropolis of Ch'ang-an fell into ruins after the collapse of Han, and during the age of division and invasion, barbarians from the north grazed their flocks in its suburbs. But it was revived in all its glory under the splendid medieval monarchs of T'ang.

To a foreign visitor this new Ch'ang-an must have seemed the most dazzling metropolis in the world. Indeed the medieval city can only be compared to Babylon, Alexandria and Rome in their greatest days. It was laid out in beautiful symmetry—a model of the land of the gods, a paradise on earth. The city was structured in accordance with the divine plan, in the form of a rectangle orientated according to the cardinal directions. It was subdivided into smaller squares by its grid of streets, the major ones leading to ceremonial gateways, named in accordance with the symbolism of the Five Activities. The gateways faced the four sacred mountains, the most important of them opening towards the south, the holy direction symbolized by *yang*, red and summer—the special direction of the Son of Heaven himself.

Ch'ang-an stretched about six miles from east to west and about five miles north to south and was protected by a wall 17 and one half feet high, built of rammed earth faced with brick and ashlar. The basic grid consisted of 25 broad carriage-ways flanked by drainage ditches, and hemmed at some times by fruit trees, at others by elm and pagoda trees. All the chief north-south streets were more than 480 feet wide—Regent Street in London is about 100 feet wide. It was traversed by many canals, some of them quite large, and all connecting with the river Wei, which brought goods from all over the empire.

Except for two large market areas in the eastern and western parts of the city, the palace complex in the north and some smaller areas taken over by the government or religious establishments, all the spaces between the streets were occupied by residential wards. These were surrounded by low walls with gates that were locked at the evening curfew, and each ward had its maze of lanes and alleys that passed among the houses, the neighbourhood shops and the service establishments.

It is thought that Ch'ang-an had about two million inhabitants in the first half of the eighth century, during the golden years of Emperor Li Lung-chi. Among them were large numbers of imperial guards, monks and nuns, as well as many foreigners, both visitors and residents, including Turks, Tibetans, Sogdians, Arabs and Persians. The population thinned out towards the south, where there were open fields, private parks and burial grounds with their shrines.

There were many magnificent buildings, both public and private. These included the residences of the great nobles, fantastically large and extravagantly furnished. At one time there were 64 magnificent Buddhist monasteries, 27 Buddhist nunneries, 10 Taoist monasteries and 6 Taoist nunneries, four Zoroastrian temples (chiefly for the use of Persian expatriates), a Manichean temple and a Nestorian Christian church.

The palace enclosure was a city in itself called "Great Luminous Palace"—a name reminiscent of the ancient "Luminous Hall". It was built on a majestic height called "Dragon Head Plain", from which it overlooked the rest of the city. The complex was approached by a bluish stone-paved road that curved in the form of a dragon's tail. Within the complex were great basilicas for formal audiences and every sort of lesser structure, ranging from pleasure pavilions to libraries and archives. There were artistically landscaped lakes, which reflected weeping willows and many coloured flowers; there were private shrines, barracks and even such amenities as a polo field. Below the palace enclosure to the south was a grand vista of the chess-board city, and far off beyond it lay the blue southern hills where the great noblemen had their country villas.

To most medieval Chinese a journey to Ch'ang-an was a holy pilgrimage. This was the city of the divine king, and the ascent to the sacred palace on its dragon hill—like a paradise on the summit of a holy mountain—was an enactment of the journey of the human soul to the mountain of the gods. This theme of the journey of the released soul to a mountain paradise is as old as Chinese literature. In Han times, the philosopher Wang Ch'ung had noted the common opinion that "seeing the god-king in a dream is in fact the soul's ascent to Heaven; ascent to Heaven is like the ascent of a mountain". The Great Luminous Palace of T'ang brought the old dream down to earth.

Like other man-made replicas of the unseen, supernatural world, the Great Luminous Palace on its miniature world-mountain was perishable. Early in A.D. 904, after a quarter of a century of civil war, the powerful war lord Chu Ch'üan-chung brought the T'ang Dynasty to an end and transferred the capital to Loyang. The great mansions and palace buildings of Ch'ang-an, ravaged by arson and pillage, were dismantled, and their timbers floated down stream to the new capital. Massive walls were demolished; beautiful water parks were allowed to silt up.

For generations afterwards, the site of the great capital provided a theme for melancholy reflection by poets on the transience of human glory. Wei Chuang, who lived during the fall of T'ang, wrote:

Filling my eyes—walls and doorways, where herbs of spring are deep.
Wounded times! wounded affairs! even more—wounded hearts!
The carriage wheels, the horses' traces—where are they now?
At the twelve towers of jade they are nowhere to be found.

But the idea of an earthly paradise did not die out. Though the splendid palaces passed away, men continued to build gardens that also represented the cosmic order, though on a much smaller scale.

A garden represented two worlds simultaneously—the physical and the spiritual. Stones and water were the essential components used to portray the physical world. Stones were analogous to the human skeletal structure and water corresponded to vitalizing blood and breath; stones and water together represented the anatomy of the earth. At the same time, a garden was a model of the paradises of the gods on their incredibly remote hilltops, and the trees and flowering shrubs planted in them symbolized the world-trees and gem-trees that ornamented those distant Edens.

The earliest Chinese gardens of which we have any knowledge are those of the kings and great lords of Chou. They seem to have been stocked with every sort of bird and beast, and were at once hunting parks, zoological gardens, places for recreation, and magical symbols. That a king could hunt animals from all over his realm in this limited space signified that all the creatures of the world were in his power. An ancient ode to Wen Wang, founder of Chou, describes such a scene:

The king is in the holy park,
Where doe and hart are cowering;
Doe and hart are sleek and spruce,
White birds shimmer and shine.
The king is at the holy pond:
At its brim the fish are leaping.

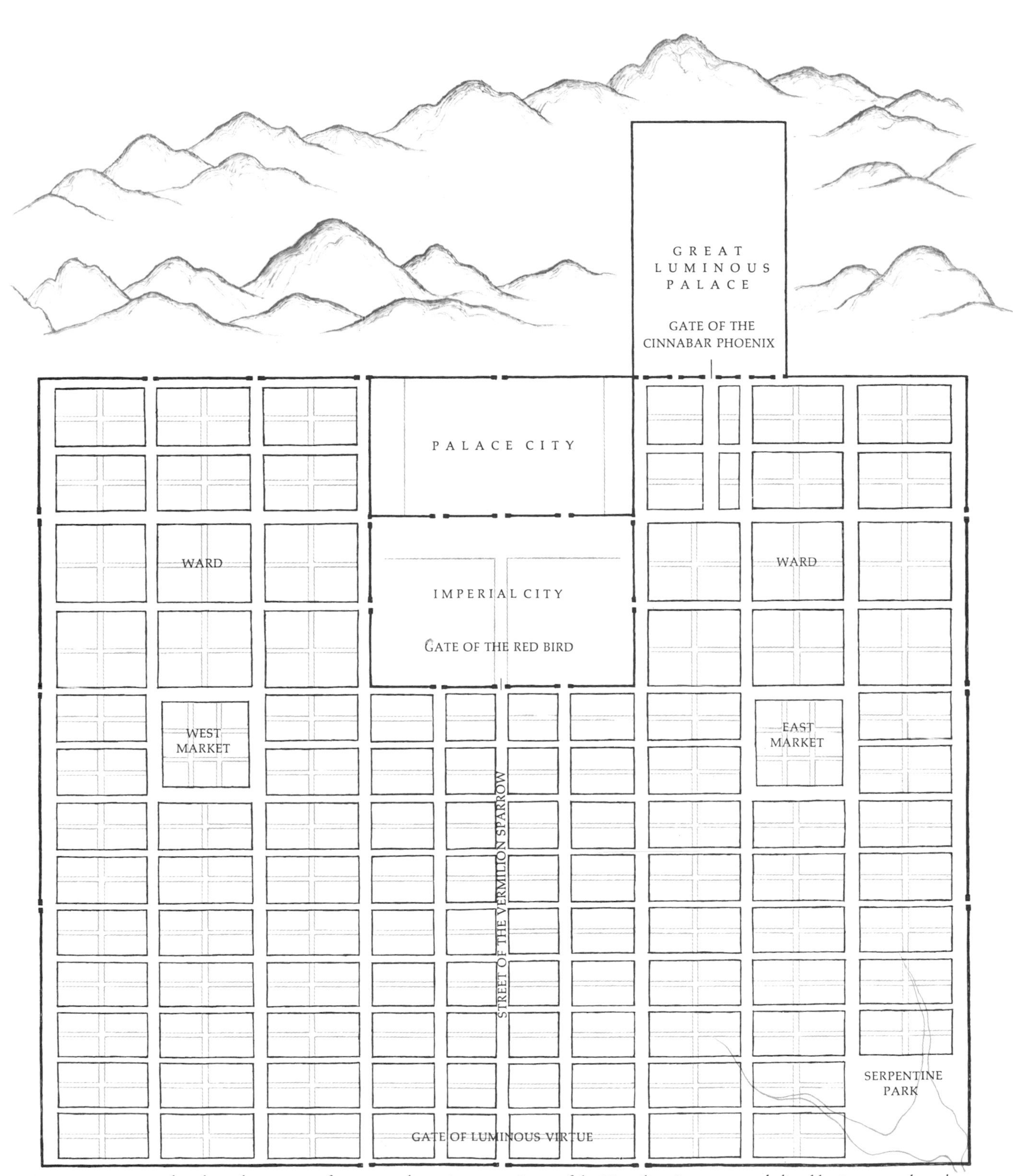

THE DIVINE PLAN, *based on the concept of a rectangular universe, is reflected in the grid layout of the T'ang capital, Cha'ng-an. Covering some 30 square miles, the city was divided into residential wards, two main markets and several parks. Visitors entered from the south, the holy direction; the main thoroughfare, the Street of the Vermilion Sparrow, symbolized by its name the colour and animal associated with the south. This street led to the Imperial City, reserved for government buildings, and the Palace City, part of the royal household. North-east of the city, set among hills, was the Great Luminous Palace, the emperor's home.*

The greatest garden of Han times was the huge hunting park of the monarch Liu Ch'e outside the capital of Ch'ang-an; it is described in the poems of Chang Heng and other Han writers as a gigantic model of the empire. The park was a virtual museum containing specimens of every beautiful animal, plant and stone in the Chinese world; it was the emperor's realm in miniature and symbolized the vast domain that owed him allegiance. The major rivers of the Middle Kingdom, stocked with fine fishes, were re-created there and even specimens of economic minerals were on display. The great holy mountains were represented too, duplicated by masses of rock and earth.

It was not until the period of division and invasion after the fall of Han in the third century A.D. that the idea of a garden as a place for spiritual enrichment through intimate communion with natural beauty began to appear. At that time, some men, bemused by thoughts of the artificiality and transience of public life and inspired by Buddhist and Taoist ideas about nature, were conceiving of gardens as simpler affairs, not much different from bits of unspoiled wilderness. This view was encouraged by new experiences of travellers and emigrants to the south; there they began to appreciate a greener, lusher and warmer environment than they had ever known. Between the Han and T'ang periods a profound feeling for real trees and rocks and birds and flowers had been developing among sensitive men. No longer were they considered only as symbols of cosmic forces; they were thought of as living and even lovable creatures. In late T'ang times the climax of these tendencies was seen in the development of the wild, romantic garden.

Most influential in creating this taste was the ninth-century magnate Li Te-yü, a man of solitary temperament who devoted what time he could to writing and to his gardens. His urban garden in Ch'ang-an was renowned for its strangely shaped stones and gnarled pines that were becoming the vogue among gardeners and painters. But his greatest pride was his country garden in the hills south of the eastern capital of Loyang, which was described by a contemporary writer as a veritable paradise, a suitable residence for godlike beings. Within its three-mile periphery it contained specimens from every part of the empire—many of them new and exotic plants such as magnolias, camellias, the crimson-berried nandin and the rare golden larch. He also kept birds and rare stones there and his great pride was a replica of the gorges of the river Yangtze. The great man justified his interest in these as necessary for a poet, who must be accurate when dealing with nature.

An innovation for which Li Te-yü was largely responsible was the transformation of the miniature world-mountain, a basic element of the garden, from a mound of earth and rubble to a single huge stone. He loved rocks of fantastic and even grotesque contours, especially water-worn, perforated limestone, and because of his influence the chief attraction of many a ninth-century garden became a massive, twisted rock representing a Taoist mountain paradise.

Gradually, the Chinese garden was being perfected, its representation of the cosmic diagram reflecting more and more the multiplicity and subtleties of the real world. And yet the old idea of a garden paradise persisted.

To the talented Buddhist painter and poet of the tenth century, Kuan-hsiu, mountains were still crystalline palaces and earthly gardens were still paradises of the gods. Describing an actual garden, glowing with rare blossoms, he wrote: "The peach flowers seem to open up on a palace of the sylphs". The dream of an earthly garden of the spirit lived on after kings and their sacred halls and cosmic parks had vanished.

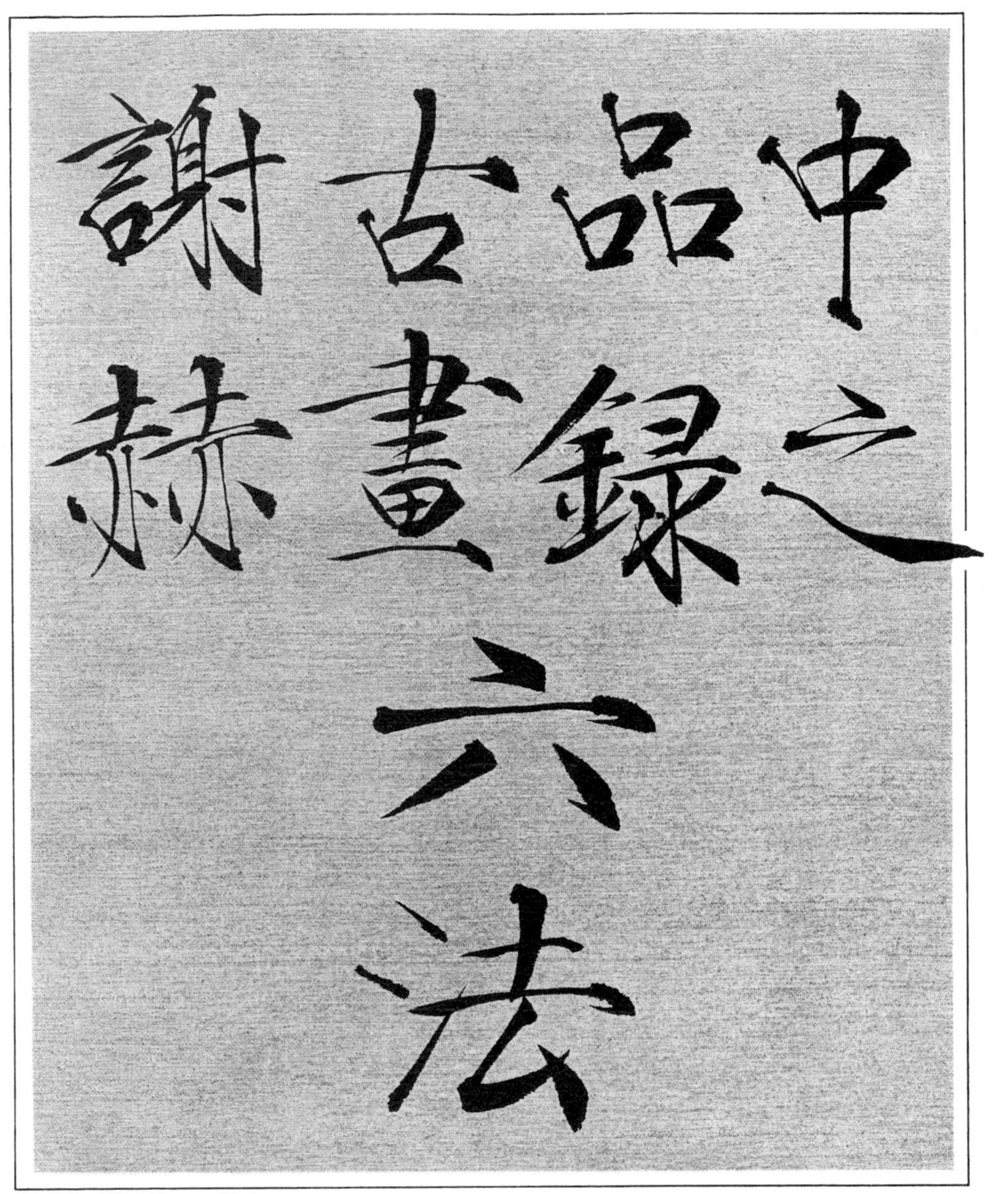

CALLIGRAPHY, *proclaiming "Hsieh Ho's Six Canons of Painting", reflects the linear grace of Chinese art.*

THE LANGUAGE OF PAINTING

The painters of Ancient China, swiftly brushing ink and water-colours on silk, were not content merely to imitate nature. They set themselves a more elusive and challenging goal: to capture the spirit as well as the form of their subjects. According to the influential fifth-century art critic, Hsieh Ho, a painter needed to fulfil six canons to be a truly great artist. His rules, which are elaborated upon in the following pages, called for a high degree of skill in composition, colour rendition and especially brushwork—a technique closely related to the picture-language of Chinese writing. But most important of all, Hsieh Ho demanded an infusion of the artist's own spirit to give the painting *ch'i*—the vitality of life itself.

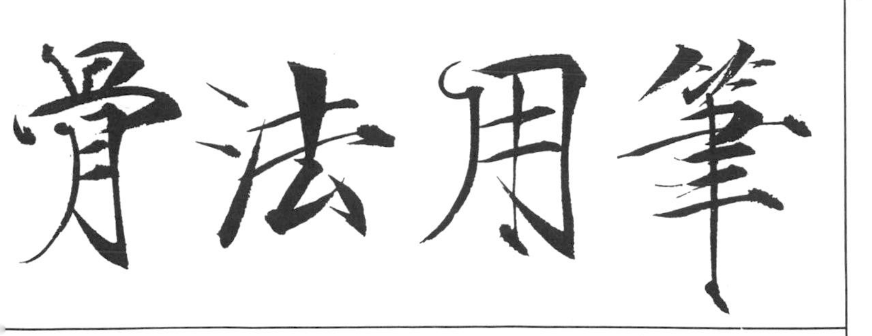

DEFT BRUSH-WORK

To Chinese artists, line—rather than the light and shadow of much Western art—was the basic structural element of all painting, as it was of calligraphy. A high premium was placed on the skilled manipulation of the brush, which was made of a bone or wood handle fitted with unusually soft, flexible bristles. In the calligraphy above, done with such a brush, one of Hsieh Ho's primary canons of art is expressed in the four Chinese ideograms "Structure-Method Use-Brush". Indeed, the mastering of brush-work was considered so necessary in giving life to a painting that one art critic described the brush as an extension of "the arm, the belly and the mind"; another called brush-work an artist's "heart-print".

Like calligraphers, Chinese painters practised for years to develop the muscular control necessary to execute swift, delicate strokes. Every artist tried to perfect his brush-work until it bore an imprint as personal as his handwriting. When a painter had mastered this technique, his strokes were said to resemble a dance—full of energy, movement and life. As one master put it, brush-strokes should be "like a flock of birds darting out of the forest, or like a frightened snake disappearing in the grass, or like the cracks in a shattered wall".

DYNAMIC LINES *animate two Chinese gentlemen portrayed on a third-century ceramic tile (left). Curved lines of varying widths impart a feeling of movement as the men engage in conversation.*

CALLIGRAPHY'S INFLUENCE *on painting is seen in the facile brush-strokes that depict the face (detail, right above) of one of the men on the tile. The main lines of the painting were done with the same kind of quick, fluid motions as the calligraphic symbols shown on the right, and both have the desired quality of "life".*

應物象形

ACCURATE LIKENESSES

FAITHFULLY RENDERED FORMS *make this record of a Court party, painted a thousand years ago, bubble with life. Its carefully drawn women with their delicate, flowered robes are both convincing and graceful. The painter's masterful eye for detail is indicated by his treatment of the pug-like dog lying under the table (above).*

The purpose of the painter was, in the words of an artist of the fourth century, "to portray the spirit through the form". The ability to draw good likenesses was gradually learned over the centuries. By the ninth century, when works like the Court scene below were being painted, artists more than satisfied the stipulation of Hsieh Ho's canon, which is symbolized on the left by the characters "Fidelity-Type Depict-Form".

This canon, however, became the focus of a continuing debate among Chinese artists and critics. Which was more important: exact representation or free expression? Virtually all artists agreed that the subject of a painting should have recognizable form, but many felt that the spirit of the subject was even more important. One ninth-century critic, striking at the root of the problem, declared that an artist who could capture life necessarily had to be adept at representation—but that a good representationalist could not always capture life.

VERSATILE COLOURS

Through the T'ang Dynasty colour played a major role in Chinese painting, and in the Buddhist art of that period it achieved a brightness and variety it would never approach again. In the canon above ("According-Object Apply-Colour"), Hsieh Ho insisted that the colours of a painting match the hues of nature. While most artists followed this dictum, others went beyond it, particularly in religious art. In the Buddhist painting on the left, for example, colour was used symbolically to represent the forces of nature. Thus green, red, yellow, white and black stood for wood, fire, earth, metal and water respectively. In another Buddhist work (*right*), colour performed more purely decorative purposes, creating a dazzling mosaic of the primary colours of red, blue and yellow, and the softer secondary colours of violet, green and orange.

After the 10th century, however, an increasing interest in landscape painting led to a decline in strong colours; they were not suited to nature's real hues, and artists also felt that they obscured fine brush-work. In place of brilliant pigments, painters began to use delicate ink-washes, giving the linear outlines of forms more prominence. Ultimately, many artists gave up colour altogether, believing that the contrast between black and white portrayed more effectively the opposites of nature.

A SACRED WORK (*left*) *represents the Kuan-yin, a Buddhist deity, surrounded by other divine figures and mystical symbols. At the bottom are portrayed the patrons who commissioned the work.*

A BRILLIANT PANORAMA *in contrasting colours depicts the temptation and assault of Buddha by the devil Mara. Stones and arrows cast at him by monstrous spirits miraculously turn to flowers.*

AN ILLUSION OF DEPTH *was achieved in this copy of an eighth-century landscape painting by arranging rocks into a series of overlapping shapes. The sketch (top) still recommended the technique almost 1,000 years later.*

A FEELING OF HEIGHT *was conveyed in the same landscape by juxtaposing a mountain and two smaller foot-hills. Instructions in the use of this compositional device appear above with another sketch from the handbook.*

WELL-PLANNED SPACE

Over the centuries, Chinese painters worked assiduously to perfect the craft of composition, which Hsieh Ho described as "Division-Planning Placing-Arranging" (*characters above*). In addition to rules laid down for arriving at the proper balance of elements in a picture, special attention was paid to achieving a sense of three-dimensional space. Perspective, in the Western sense, of a view that appeared to be seen through a window, did not lend itself to the Chinese hand-held scroll, which was unrolled and viewed in sections, not as a whole. The Chinese developed other devices for expressing distances; two major ones, as illustrated in an early Chinese scroll, are shown on the left, accompanied by schematic explanations taken from a 17th-century handbook of painting. A third set of illustrations, on this page, demonstrates how the two devices could be used to work together.

As landscape scrolls were unrolled (*next page*), variations of these compositional devices came into play. Viewers were not confined to a single, fixed viewpoint, but were treated to a constantly shifting sense of depth, height and subject-matter, as their eyes roamed across the landscape. The painting became almost like a modern motion picture as it added to space the new dimension of time.

COMBINING HEIGHT AND DEPTH, *both of the techniques shown on the opposite page are used here to give the effect of a sprawling landscape that draws the viewer's eye past the foreground cliffs to distant, towering peaks.*

VENERATED TRADITIONS

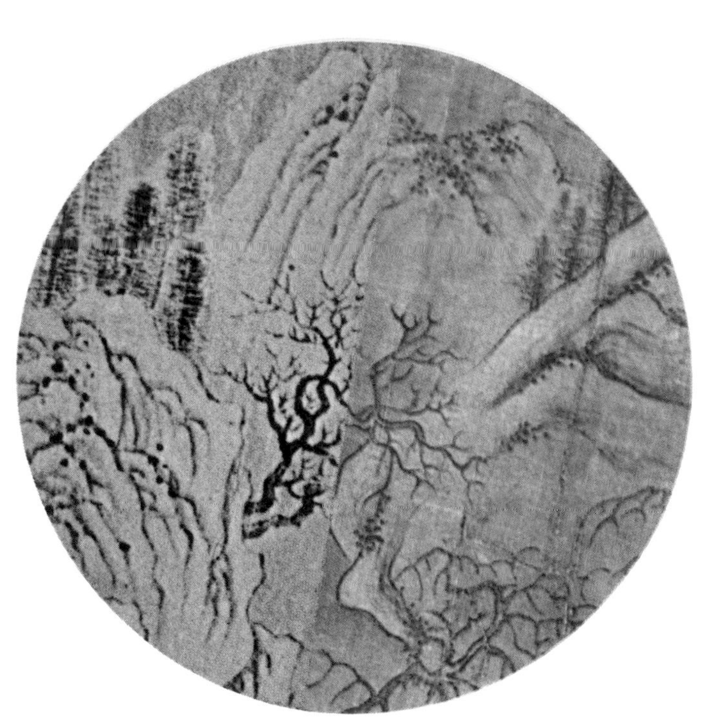

MATCHING DETAILS, *taken from the two landscape scrolls on these pages, fit together like pieces of a jigsaw puzzle. Though both works were copied from the same original, they clearly show brush-work styles of different artists in the modelling of the rocks.*

A sense of the past permeated art, and copying great artists of earlier times was considered an important and honourable endeavour. In the characters above Hsieh Ho urged artists to master this skill as a means of "transmitting the past". Copying not only showed reverence for what had gone before; it also had the practical function of putting valuable paintings into wider circulation, while training the hand and eye of the young artist. Since it was believed that the ancient masters had found an ideal way of expressing form for every type of object, the artist, by copying these established forms, became free to concentrate on giving "life" to his painting.

In copying, the Chinese did not limit themselves to reproducing slavish replicas. Indeed, they believed that exact duplication lost the essential ingredient of spontaneity. To bring reproductions alive in a new way, they frequently attempted free variations on traditional themes. For example, the 16th-century landscape scroll below and the 15th-century one on the right are both copies of the same eighth-century original, but each copyist has injected his own creative touches. The long scroll in particular has new mountains, a longer river and a greater variety of trees and rocks. Most important, the artist has delineated them in his own style.

A RENOWNED LANDSCAPE *by the eighth-century master Wang Wei, famed for its subtle handling of space, is shown in this copy by a later artist. It was probably traced from the original work, entitled "Clearing After Snowfall on the Mountains Along the River".*

EXTENSIVE ADDITIONS *to the Wang Wei landscape appear in a copy made free-hand some 600 years later. The work has been extended into a sweeping view of the river, and the spacing of elements and the rendering of rocks are noticeably the artist's own.*

氣韻生動

LIFELIKE SPIRIT

To the Chinese, the one attribute that distinguished great art was the mysterious quality of "vitality", defined by Hsieh Ho, in the characters above, as "Breath-Resonance Life-Motion". Unlike craftsmanship, which could be learned by mastering the lessons in the five preceding canons of art, the ability to impart life to a painting could not be taught. It was considered a gift from Heaven itself—a gift that put its possessor in harmony with the world, enabling him to perceive and re-create the inherent spirit of his subject.

The eighth-century painter Wang Wei—a master who possessed this gift—described pictures that had succeeded in capturing life on a still, flat surface: "The wind rises from the green forest, and the foaming water rushes in the stream. Alas! Such painting cannot be achieved by physical movements of the fingers and hand, but only by the spirit entering into them. This is the nature of painting".

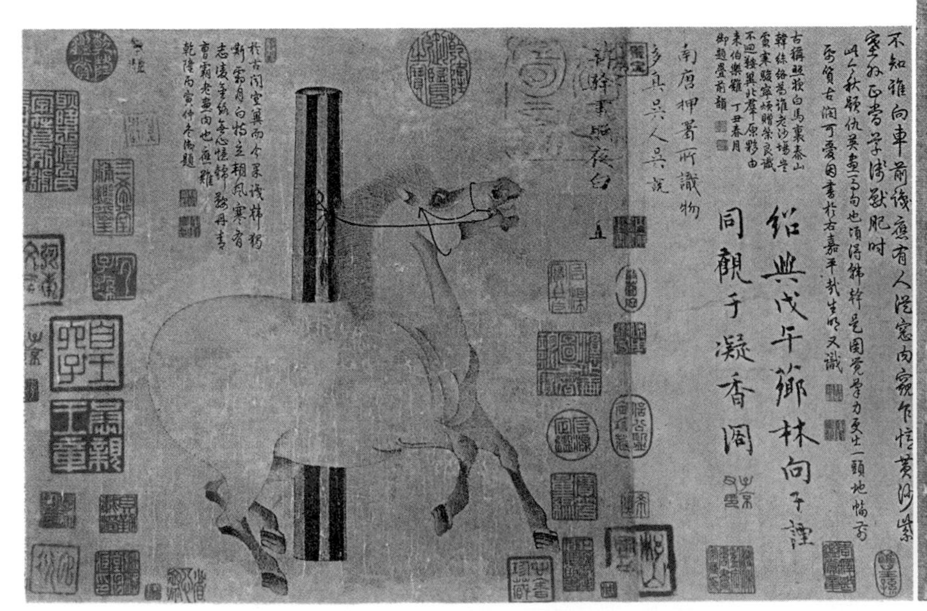

A REARING STEED *fights its tether in this lifelike copy of an eighth-century masterpiece.*

A CONTEMPLATIVE SCHOLAR *lives on in this copy o*

irited portrait of the eighth century. The original is attributed to Wang Wei, who of all Chinese painters was thought best able to impart the quality of vitality.

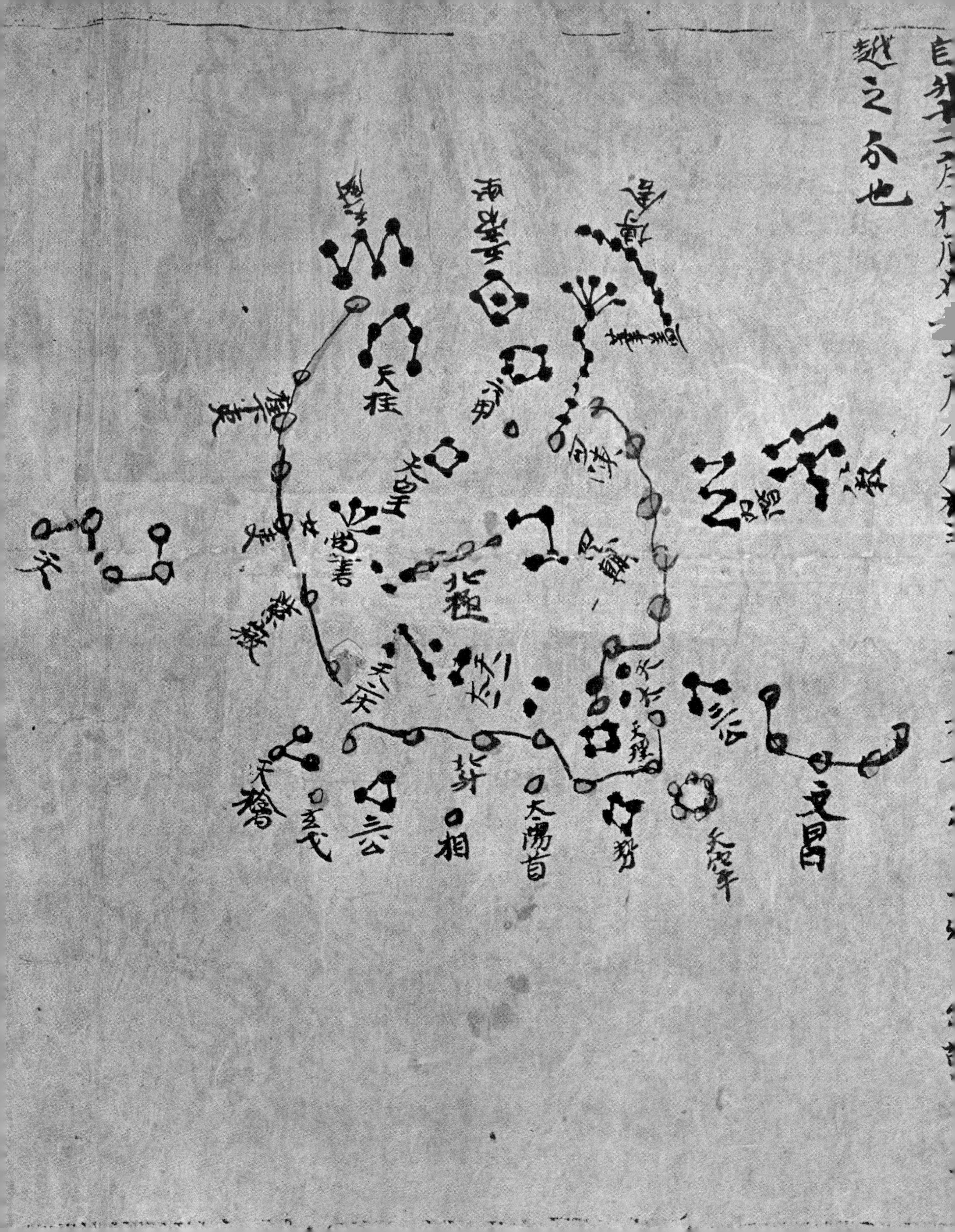

越之分也
天柱
北極
尚書
文昌
三公
相
太陽首
勢
天牢
玄戈
天槍

6

DISCOVERERS AND INVENTORS

MAPPING THE SKIES, *Ch'ien Le-chih, a fifth-century astronomer, charted the constellations, using colours to associate them with the men who had determined their positions. The Big Dipper (bottom) is said to have been identified by the shaman Hsien of the Shang period (1500–1000* B.C.*).*

The men of Ancient China searched earth and sky to discover the truth about the world and its workings, yet they would have been baffled by the idea of "pure science". They did not probe the unknown for whatever unsuspected truths might still lie hidden there. They did not carry out experiments uncommitted to specific goals, but directed their probings mainly towards rediscovery of the supposedly reliable methods of ancient masters. "Free inquiry" would have seemed meaningless to them.

The ancient Chinese explored the mysteries of nature for one of three reasons: to add the weight of new evidence to what they already believed, to refine existing techniques or to attain more effectively such pre-established goals as a more accurate astrology or a more effective alchemy. The purpose of understanding the natural order was to stabilize the social order based on it or to accommodate one's personal life more closely to it. Subsidiary to this great aim was the more homely, technological one—the improvement of the skills needed to increase wealth or comfort, as by finding ways to make more efficient ploughs or less fragile dishes.

From the earliest days, astronomy was the queen of Chinese sciences. The ancient Chinese assiduously studied the sky to perfect their methods of astrological predictions; for many centuries the study of astronomy remained a royal monopoly, delegated only to the keenest observers and the most dedicated mathematicians, native and foreign. It was believed that knowledge of astronomy gave power over man and nature and hence should be kept from ordinary persons. Even as late as the eighth century A.D., harsh penalties were imposed on any private citizen who owned or used astronomical instruments or charts of the sky, or who consulted cosmic diagrams and prognostic books.

Legend says that the prototype of the astronomical observatory was the tower of Wen Wang, founder of the Chou lineage, before 1000 B.C.:

> *He designed, he inaugurated a holy platform—*
> *Designed it, laid it out.*
> *The common folk built it—*
> *By day's end achieved it!*

From such structures as Wen Wang's legendary tower, the Bronze Age astrologers observed and recorded the seemingly irregular paths of the planets, searched for dragons in the flickering Northern Lights and worried about sun-spots—those mysterious splotches that appeared at unpredictable times on the face of the sun. All were thought to convey divine messages for men's guidance.

The measurements and reverent calculations of the royal astronomers provided the basis for the imperial almanac, the origins of which may go back to the earliest times. The almanac fixed the lengths of the months, determined the dates of the spring and autumn equinoxes—the two times a year that night and day are of equal length—and of the summer and winter solstices—when night and day differ most in length.

The most difficult problem to the astronomers plotting the almanac was the determination of the length of the solar year—that is, the exact length of time required to complete the cycle of seasons. The ancient estimation had been that it was 366 days; this figure was corrected to 365 1/4 days by the fourth century B.C. and this calculation was constantly refined after that. The Chinese based many of their computations not on the sun but on the position of the pole-star and the wheeling around it of circumpolar constellations like the Big Dipper; its handle, pointing north in winter, south in summer, marked off the 12 months of the Chinese year. The movement of the planet Jupiter, which was called the "Year Star" and whose orbit takes 12 years to complete, was also taken into account in the Chinese division of time into periods. Finally, the phases of the moon, from dark to full, which bear no fixed relationship to the solar year, had to be included in the computations so that the calendar months could be adjusted to fit the year.

The indispensable function of the calendar was to set the date of the New Year—when all life began anew. That most important day in the calendar, the day from which all others were counted, was the winter solstice, considered the head of the year. Then the positive, warming yang force was thought to be at its lowest ebb, about to reassert itself to bring the welcome spring. Since the sun was often covered by clouds on that critical day, the official astronomers determined when it fell by making a projection from the summer solstice, which they fixed by watching the shadow of a special stone pillar about eight feet tall. When the shadow was shortest, they knew that the summer solstice had arrived.

The ancient Chinese did not distinguish meteorological events—those that occur in the vicinity of the earth—from the astronomical—those occurring in outer space. To them all were events in the sky. The distinction they made was between those, such as the swing of a constellation around the pole-star, that reflected the regular and predictable side of nature, and those, such as sun-spots, that were irregular and unpredictable and were considered heaven-sent portents for wise men to interpret. Because such interpretations were held to be of the utmost importance, the Chinese left uniquely complete accounts of these events.

Their records of the occurrence of sun-spots—which were often made easily observable when northern China dust storms dimmed the solar glare—are enlightening today. The accounts of comets in China, which are more complete than those made anywhere else in the ancient world, still form the basis for computing the orbits of such comets as Halley's, which was observed first in China in 240 B.C.

Records of eclipses of the sun and the moon, including some that must have been reported from outlying regions, have been found on Shang oracle bones, inscribed seven centuries before the first Babylonian eclipse records were made. Eclipses were mentioned in the Chou classics, and from the third century B.C. on they were systematically recorded.

Attempts to predict them began in that century, but despite steady improvement, no truly reliable method was worked out.

Legend says that the stars were first catalogued by a shaman named Hsien more than 3,000 years ago in Shang times. The first star-mappers whose records remain were Shih Shen and Kan Te of the fourth century B.C. The stars they identified, along with those supposedly identified by the legendary Shang shaman, were incorporated into later maps. The luck of all three Chinese astronomers was better than that of the Babylonian Naburianna and the Greek Timocharis, whose sky charts have quite disappeared. A 10th-century version of the map of Ch'ien Le-chih, who worked in the fifth century A.D., has recently been discovered. The oldest extant scientific star map, it shows the stars of shaman Hsien in white, those of Shih Shen in red and those of Kan Te in black.

Of all stars, the most remarkable—and the most ominous—to the Chinese were the supernovae: large, brilliant stars that appeared miraculously where no stars had been seen before. The unique Chinese records of those "new stars", or "stranger stars", have excited the interest of 20th-century astronomers; there is nothing of comparable antiquity which explains these mysterious cosmic explosions, some of which may have occurred at the time the universe was born, but so far away from the earth that their light is only now reaching us.

The Chinese invention most important to astronomy was a fundamental tool, the armillary sphere. This outstanding product of Han culture was essentially a nest of rings—hoops that represented imaginary circles dividing up the sky for measurement and mapping. Each ring was marked off for use as a gauge. The most important one was the equatorial armil, a bronze ring representing the celestial equator, which is an imaginary line that divides the sky in two above the earth's equator. The Chinese called this ring the "Gauge of the Red Road". Its invention is attributed to Keng Shou-Ch'ang, an astronomer of the first century B.C., but it is possibly much older. Combined with a bronze tube through which heavenly bodies were watched, its graduated rings allowed for more accurate location of the positions of the sun, moon and planets with reference to the celestial equator. But the true motions of these bodies could be worked out accurately only with reference to the ecliptic —the plane of the earth's orbit round the sun— not the equator, and another great advance came with the addition of an ecliptical armil to the equatorial armil in the first century A.D.

This second bronze hoop, called "Gauge of the Yellow Road", was particularly helpful in calculating the expected dates of eclipses—a matter of primary concern, since eclipses were very portentous occurrences. The Gauge of the Yellow Road also improved computations of planetary motions, but the Chinese results, not being based on sound geometry, remained inferior to those of the Greeks.

In the fourth century, Yü Hsi discovered that the equinoxes appear about 20 minutes earlier each year—a frightening and subversive idea to believers in an unaltering universe. The discovery of this steady change—or "precession"—of the equinoxes was made possible by the fully developed armillary sphere: a nest of bronze rings that served as a miniature skeleton of the cosmos. It is believed that the first one was built in the second century A.D. by Chang Heng, astronomer and poet. His brilliant invention was cast in bronze in A.D. 124 and was little more than a yard in diameter. Its four graduated armillary rings represented the equator, the ecliptic, the meridian—an imaginary line that circles the earth over the poles—and the horizon. It was called "Gauge of the Enveloping Sky", a name that implied that the astronomers believed that the sky was no mere umbrella-like

APPLYING A PAINFUL CURE, *a village doctor ignites clumps of grass powder on the back of a patient, who must be held down by friends. Everyone in this 12th-century painting, even the doctor's assistant standing on the right, cringes at the treatment.*

hemisphere, as conservative tradition held, but was an all-encompassing sphere.

Chang Heng, it seems, was also the first man to design and build an orrery—a reduced model of the armillary sphere rotated mechanically by water power, the individual rings moving in imitation of the motions of the heavenly bodies. Here was the indispensable mechanism of a modern clock in embryo. Later, more intricately contrived orreries were ornamented with miniature planets, an image of the Big Dipper, and figures of the 28 "mansions" of the moon, the segments of the sky through which the moon was presumed to travel.

Finally, in the eighth century, the learned Buddhist monk I-hsing and the military engineer Liang Ling-tsan, trying to devise a more precise calendar, constructed a great astronomical clock on the grounds of the palace in Ch'ang-an. This ancestor of all modern clocks, completed in A.D. 721, was the first machine known to employ an escapement, the basic device that is still used to regulate clocks. It divided the power from a water-wheel into exactly similar unit impulses so that the apparent motions of stars and the less regular wanderings of the planets could be duplicated by the measurable movements of a bronze microcosm of rings and little spheres, while wooden figures struck out the sequence of the hours.

The extent of the influence of other countries' astronomers on the early Chinese is still not known. It is suspected that some ideas of the scientists of Mesopotamia were dimly known during the classical age in the Far East—for example, the astrological concept of the 28 mansions of the moon. The advent of Buddhism and its paraphernalia of Indian learning, including mathematics and astronomical theory, had some effect on official Chinese astronomy. Greek ideas also reached China by way of India. In the early centuries of our era foreign treatises were gradually translated into Chinese, and finally, during the early eighth century, Indian astronomers monopolized the researches of the T'ang imperial observatories.

The most notable of these foreign specialists was Gautama Siddharta, under whose name an astrological almanac was published in A.D. 729. The almanac embodied the most advanced methods of computation, including the use of a significant new number, zero. Men like Siddharta represent the high tide of Indian intellectual domination in the Far East. But although Indian astronomy and mathematics influenced such inquiring, receptive minds as the T'ang monk I-hsing—who not only helped to build the first clock, but also refined the estimate of the period of Jupiter's year—they had little permanent influence on the established routine of the Chinese astronomers.

After astronomy, alchemy was a major preoccupation of the Chinese. Its prime goal was the discovery of a potion that would confer immortality. In their pursuit of this aim, the Chinese made important contributions to the healing arts, especially in the field of pharmacology.

Chinese alchemists, influenced by the Taoist belief in the transmutability of all substances, believed that if they could discover a method of turning base metals into gold—which lasted for ever—they would at the same time have discovered the elixir of life. To them the Taoist theory of the interchangeability of substances seemed to have been verified by the apparent transmutation of lead into silver during the smelting of galena ore, of long-buried ice into rock crystal, of shining stars into stony meteorites and of living, breathing creatures into stone fossils. They believed that these changes were caused by a universal underlying process, which, if it could be discovered, could be controlled and accelerated in a laboratory.

Li Shao-chün is the first alchemist mentioned in

early Chinese records. Pretending to immense age, he came to the Court of Emperor Liu Ch'e in the second century B.C. He told the ruler that a Taoist goddess, the Spirit of the Furnace, who was a beautiful woman clothed in red, had shown him how to convert cinnabar—a red mercuric ore—into gold. Prolonged life would be the reward, he said, of the man who ate from dishes made of that divine gold. The emperor, who was obsessed with a desire for immortality, must have supplied a laboratory and the cinnabar.

The earliest surviving purely alchemical book, the *Ts'an t'ung Ch'i*, was written in later Han times. Unfortunately it is couched in quite esoteric language and could serve as a laboratory manual only to the trained initiate; mercury was called "dragon", lead was called "tiger", and other substances bore similar names. The book contains the traditional alchemical notions—gold can be made from cinnabar, the eating of refined mercury compounds prolongs life—but it also describes such scientifically accurate processes as the reduction of white lead—basic lead carbonate—to lead metal by the use of carbon.

The most famous of all students of alchemy was Ko Hung. His ideas are preserved in the book *Pao P'u Tzu*, which he wrote late in the fourth century A.D., after years of wandering far from the disturbed northern plains in search of peace in the politically untroubled south. His volume treats of many kinds of Taoist lore—such as instructions for writing charms and spells, and the secret names of forest goblins—but it is mainly devoted to the prime alchemical purposes: the creation of gold and of the elixir of life.

He describes the proper conditions for alchemical labours: they must be carried out in a retreat on a sacred mountain, after the alchemist has fasted and anointed himself with aromatics. Hostile presences, such as women, lechers and unbelievers, must be absolutely excluded. Then the alchemist could work productively at his iron cauldrons, copper bowls, earthenware braziers and bamboo tubes.

Ko Hung's formulas for making immortality elixirs and precious metals were, like those of his predecessors, based mainly on the supposed miraculous properties of cinnabar. His chief products were artificial metals, especially those that seemed to be gold-alloys and amalgams of cinnabar-derived mercury with copper, lead and arsenic. His book contains the first reference to "mosaic gold", a sulphide of tin, and called certain white amalgams "soft silver". With such magical "golds" and "silvers", the alchemists hoped to achieve the prolongation of life and to transmute the elements—objectives that modern scientists do not despise.

In the continuing quest for the elusive immortality elixir, the alchemists discovered, or concocted, many substances that did give them the temporary illusion of success. Thus they made major contributions to the advancement of medical knowledge.

The early study of medicine was sanctified by the venerable belief that the ancient holy shamans had the power to heal both the body and the mind. By the sixth century B.C., there were secular physicians who were no longer considered to have shamanistic powers, but even these did not reject the use of anti-demonic charms or appeals to the gods to supplement less mystical forms of therapy. By the third century B.C., at the latest, physicians had developed specializations. There were dietitians, veterinarians and specialists in external and internal medicine. The royal government was employing doctors to minister to the ailing members of the Court and also to study and describe various drugs and therapeutic methods.

Two forms of therapy devised by the ancient Chinese—acupuncture and moxibustion—were eventually to spread throughout Asia and even to enjoy fitful vogues in the West.

Acupuncture was the treatment of illness or pain by pricking the patient's body with needles at points that were believed to be connected with the visceral organs causing the physical disorder. Moxibustion, a treatment in which wicks of moxa —the pith of the Chinese wormwood—are burned at certain fixed points on the skin, was a related form of therapy. Both were based on a primitive view of anatomy and physiology.

The greatest contribution of early Chinese medical genius was to internal medicine, especially in the discovery of healing drugs. A considerable part of a long series of books on *materia medica* going back to the Han period still survives and is now being minutely examined by medical scientists and historians of culture because of the light it sheds on these early Chinese discoveries.

It is known that ancient Chinese pharmacologists were the first to discover the therapeutic properties of many herbs that are still valued: ephedra, a vegetable alkaloid, for asthma; iodine-rich seaweeds to treat goitre; ergot, a rye fungus, to alleviate uterine difficulties during childbirth. The Chinese made particular efforts to remedy vitamin-deficiency diseases, which became more and more prevalent as men of the Middle Kingdom moved into the rice-growing southlands. There they lived mainly on polished rice instead of eating a more balanced diet, and many contracted beriberi. They gave special attention to this disease, though its cause went unrecognized, and recommended such useful remedies as a gourd drink.

The ancient Chinese healers also utilized many non-herbal substances, most of them little used in the ancient West. The organs of animals proved to be efficacious remedies for various ailments, though medical scientists are only now discovering why. The vitamins in the livers and kidneys of pigs and in the eyes of sheep, though they were not identified as vitamins, improved the health of generations of medieval Chinese. Even the Chinese claims for the diuretic and stimulant properties of velvet deer horns and for the digitalis-like effect on the heart of the parotid-gland secretions of the toad have recently been substantiated.

Finally, the ancient Chinese anticipated the medical chemists of Europe by many centuries in their successful therapeutic use of minerals, such as iron and copper and even the salts of arsenic and mercury, which can be poisonous if not carefully administered. There remarkable discoveries are still being explored by modern scientists.

In spite of the excellence of the purely scientific discoveries of Ancient China, her greatest contribution to humanity was technological—the work of her artisans and technicians.

Four Chinese technological inventions of Han and medieval times laid the whole basis for the European exploration and colonization of the world:

the compass became the tool of the pioneering seafarers of Portugal, Holland and England; gunpowder enabled Europeans to subdue the lands they found; paper and printing made possible the wide dissemination of their ideologies and decrees.

By Han times, the Chinese had made compasses —spoons of loadstone, a naturally magnetic iron ore—that rotated freely on a polished board. The floating needle—magnetized by rubbing it with loadstone—was probably not invented before the T'ang period. Neither device was used for anything more scientific than to locate the most propitious site for a building or a tomb, however, until the 11th century, when it was finally applied to navigation. It may have reached Europe through the Arabs.

Gunpowder, to the medieval Chinese, was simply an aid to aesthetic pleasure. They had learned how to combine potassium nitrate with the proper proportions of charcoal and sulphur to make an explosive by the seventh century A.D. But they used it only in pyrotechnic displays to illuminate great Court and public celebrations: "fire trees", "flame flowers" and "peach blossoms" of gunpowder exploded in the sunset skies over the capital of Ch'ang-an. Apparently the Chinese did not use gunpowder in warfare, even as a simple incendiary substance for fire arrows, until the 11th century.

The invention of the first paper, which was made from tree bark, hemp, old rags and fishing nets, is attributed to one Ts'ai Lun in A.D. 105, but actual samples of earlier rag paper have been found. From the second century on, paper was used as a substitute for the silk cloth on which important and elegant messages had always been written. The crude pulp was strengthened with starch, sized with gypsum, coated with lichen-derived gelatine, stained in handsome colours—yellow was a favourite—and even polished. This whole complex technology was transmitted to western Asia in the eighth century. By the ninth century, paper had everywhere replaced the traditional papyrus from Egypt. Ultimately a new European industry was devoted to the manufacture of paper, and the parchment of medieval Christian monks became a thing of the past.

Printing from woodblocks is believed to have begun in the seventh century, though the earliest surviving printed book is a later one, a sacred Buddhist scroll from the eighth century A.D. The art developed from several techniques that were used between the fourth and seventh centuries: the stamping of textile patterns, the impressions of seals—both secular and religious—and the common practice of taking ink rubbings from stone engravings. These forerunners of printing were used mainly for religious purposes. Stone rubbings, for example, were used to duplicate the orthodox Confucianist texts and the sacred writings of the Buddhist and Taoist sages so that they could be widely disseminated among the faithful.

The material used in woodblock printing was usually pear or jujube wood, cut to the size of two book pages and smoothed and softened with paste. The matter to be printed was written on a two-page sheet of thin, transparent paper. This was spread carefully over the woodblock and rubbed so that the ink adhered to the paste. Then the woodblock cutter carved around the transferred written characters so that they stood out, raised in high relief. The printer brushed ink on the block and pressed blank sheets on to it to make the print.

There was no officially sponsored printing until the 10th century, though a century earlier the private presses of T'ang were turning out accounts of the lives of the Taoist saints, directions for Buddhist spells, pamphlets on divination and magic, almanacs and—surprisingly—dictionaries. The Court authorized the sale of the printed version of the Confucian classics in A.D. 953, and, at the very end of the 10th century, the printing of the official dynastic histories began.

The early invention of printing provided a means for the wide dissemination in China of the sort of materials that were available in the rest of the world only in manuscript, and hence could be read only by a small *élite*. The diffusion of the art of printing, like that of making gunpowder, seems to have followed the far-ranging Mongol conquests of Europe in the 14th century.

In addition to these inventions, which profoundly altered the course of world history, Chinese technology produced a wide range of significant but less dramatic innovations. Some of these were also adopted by Europeans; others were developed independently, but much later.

The wheelbarrow was a Chinese invention of the third century B.C., not known until centuries afterwards in Europe; so also was the breast-collar and harness that enabled domestic animals to pull heavy loads. Chinese technicians were the first to undertake deep bore-hole drilling—holes 2,000 feet deep were drilled in the salt mines of Szechwan in the first century A.D. The world's first suspension bridges supported by ingeniously woven bamboo cables, as well as the earliest known segmental-arch bridges, were built in China between the third and the seventh centuries A.D.

The ancestor of the modern Great Wall, which became the Eighth Wonder of the World, was constructed by the Ch'in emperor Shih Huang Ti in the third century B.C. It joined a series of smaller walls to reach a length of almost 1,500 miles. The first important canals were built soon afterwards and gradually a vast network was developed. By the eighth century A.D. it was possible to float a cargo from the river Yangtze in the south to the Yellow river in the north without reloading it.

First to discover the value of lacquer, a natural varnish obtained from a relative of the sumac, the Chinese used it to paint images on Bronze Age buildings and to preserve and decorate wooden articles, leather shoes and silk hats. Sometimes it was improved by the addition of gold dust, mother-of-pearl and red pigments. In the early centuries of our era, handsome Buddhist images were made by pressing lacquer-soaked cloths over clay models, and in medieval times marvellously designed actors' masks, representing the faces of supernatural beings, were made in the same way.

Another innovation was the domestication of the silkworm and the whole complex process of reeling silk filaments from cocoons. For many centuries only the Chinese knew how to control the whole life-cycle of the silkworm, feeding it with the leaves of white mulberry and killing whole generations before they could rupture their cocoons; they were also the sole possessors of the techniques for reeling off the long, undamaged, resilient filaments and twisting them into threads of great strength. Drawlooms were developed in China to weave these threads into richly ornamented damask.

Articles made of porcelain, also a Chinese invention, became the envy of the world in early medieval times. The Chinese had made fine pottery vessels since the Stone Age, but making porcelain required the addition to the clay of a mineral called feldspar. At first they merely applied feldspar as a glaze on the surface, but by T'ang times they had learned that the mineral could be added to the clay —before the vessels were moulded—and the mixture fired at a higher temperature to produce porcelain. Shards of the renowned T'ang porcelains have been found as far away as Mesopotamia and Africa.

These and other products of early China became so well known for their excellence that, by medieval times, the word for "Chinese" became a synonym for "superior" in many Asian languages. A distinguished ninth-century Arab author, Jahiz of Basra, wrote that while the Turks were the greatest soldiers and the Persians the best kings, the Chinese were pre-eminent among all craftsmen.

A PRINTER'S TOOLS *included (from top): paste, a rubbing pad, an ink-pan, an engraving knife and brushes.*

THE ART OF PRINTING

One of China's most important contributions to civilization was the invention of printing, a revolutionary development that took place in the eighth century, some 700 years before it appeared in Europe. Made possible by two other Chinese inventions, paper and ink, printing was at first largely confined to copying Buddhist scriptures. But within 200 years it was being used for all kinds of works, from official histories to classical texts, increasing literacy and radically transforming Chinese society. Despite the complex changes this early printing wrought, the method itself was ingeniously simple, and is still sometimes used in China today.

Drawings by Ed Young

THE FIRST STEP: SETTING UP THE PAGE

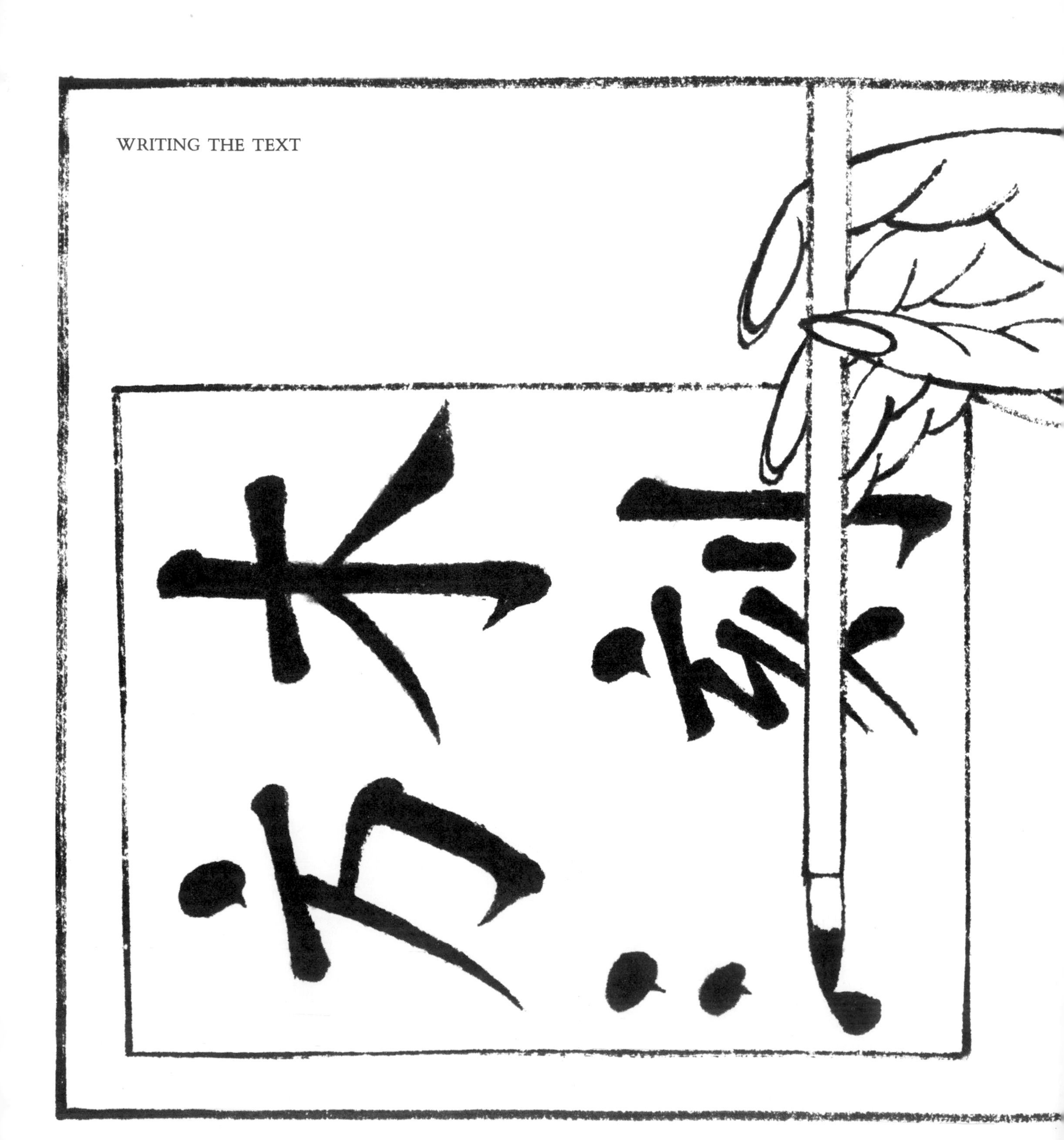

The earliest method of Chinese printing involved the use of wooden blocks, on which a text was carved in raised symbols; these symbols were then inked so that an impression of them could be transferred to paper. Sometimes printers carved individual characters on single blocks, assembling them to form the text. In this way the same block could be used again, but this advantage was limited because early Chinese writing had thousands of symbols, requiring printers to hunt through endless racks of type for each character.

In the long run, printers found it quicker and easier to carve an entire page of text on a single wooden block—the process illustrated here. First an expert calligrapher formed the characters with a brush and ink on translucent paper (*below, left*). Next, a slab of soft wood was covered with rice-paste and the paper was placed with its inked side down on the slab (*right*) to prepare for the carving process.

APPLYING PASTE AND PAPER

THE SECOND STEP: PREPARING THE BLOCK

STAINING THE WOOD

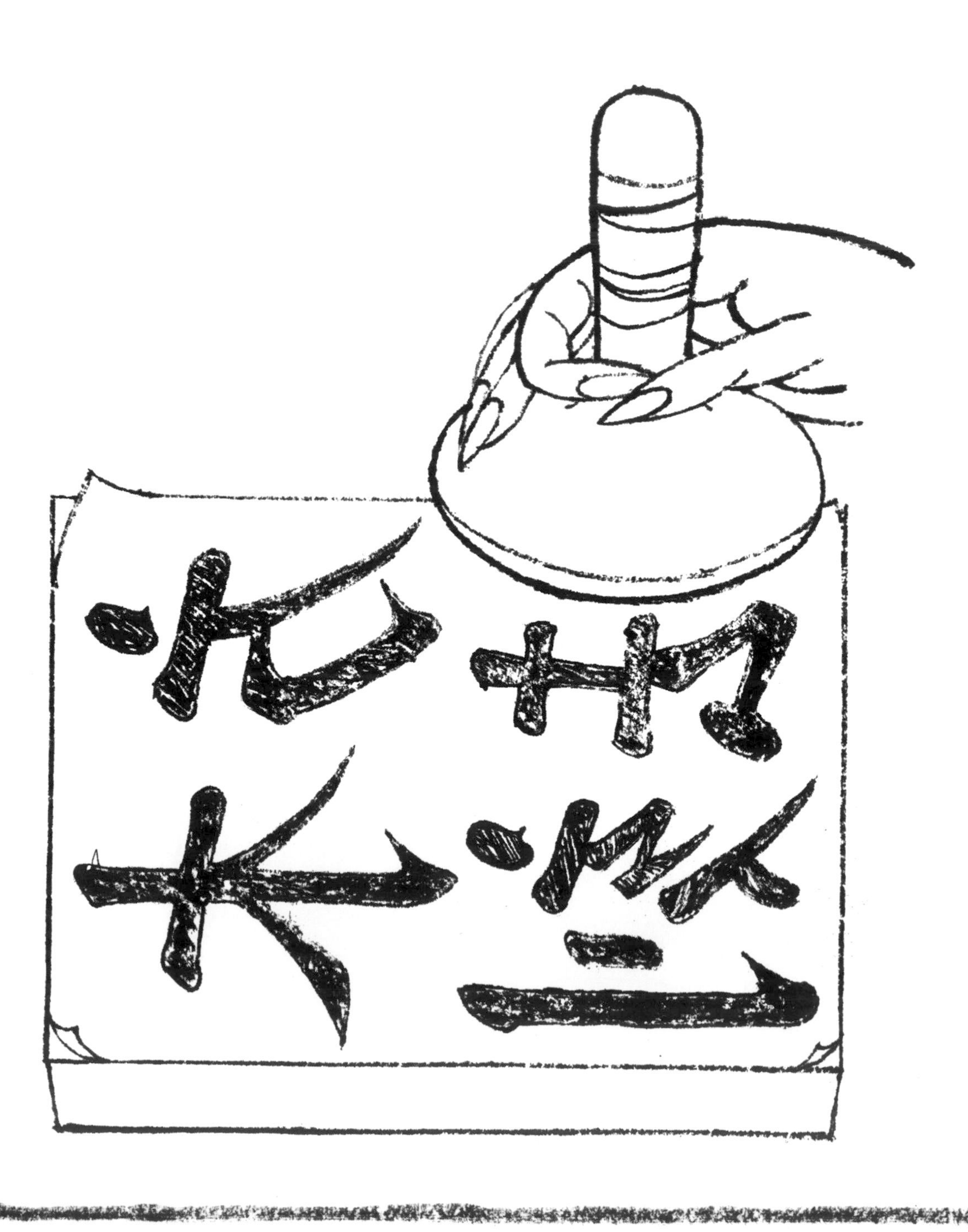

CARVING THE BLOCK

While the rice-paste held the paper on the wooden block, a block cutter rubbed the back of the paper with a rounded, cloth-covered pad (*below, left*). This caused the wet ink on the paper to stain the wood beneath. The paper was then removed and a sharp engraving tool was used to cut away all the surface of the wooden block not covered with ink (*centre*), leaving the characters as raised wood. (If the printer made a slight mistake, he simply shaped a small piece of soft wood and glued it to the block, correcting his error.)

When the block was ready for printing, the workman inked the raised characters with a brush (*right*). The best ink was made of gum mixed with lamp-black, the soot given off by burning oil; it produced a sharp impression and was almost indelible. Indeed, texts have been found which have been exposed to water for so long that the paper has become petrified, but the ink has been scarcely changed at all.

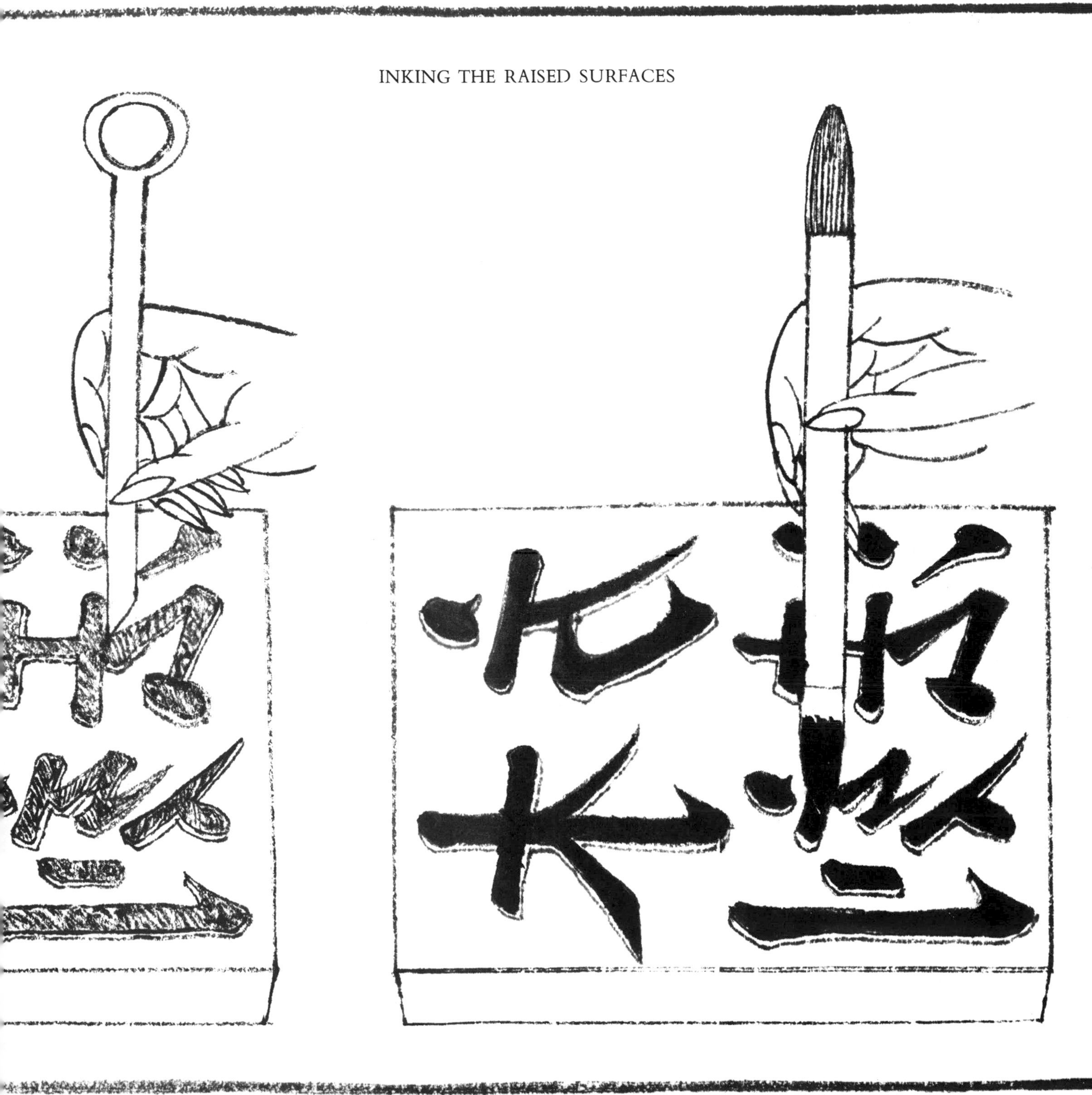

INKING THE RAISED SURFACES

THE LAST STEP: THE FINISHED PRODUCT

PRINTING THE TEXT

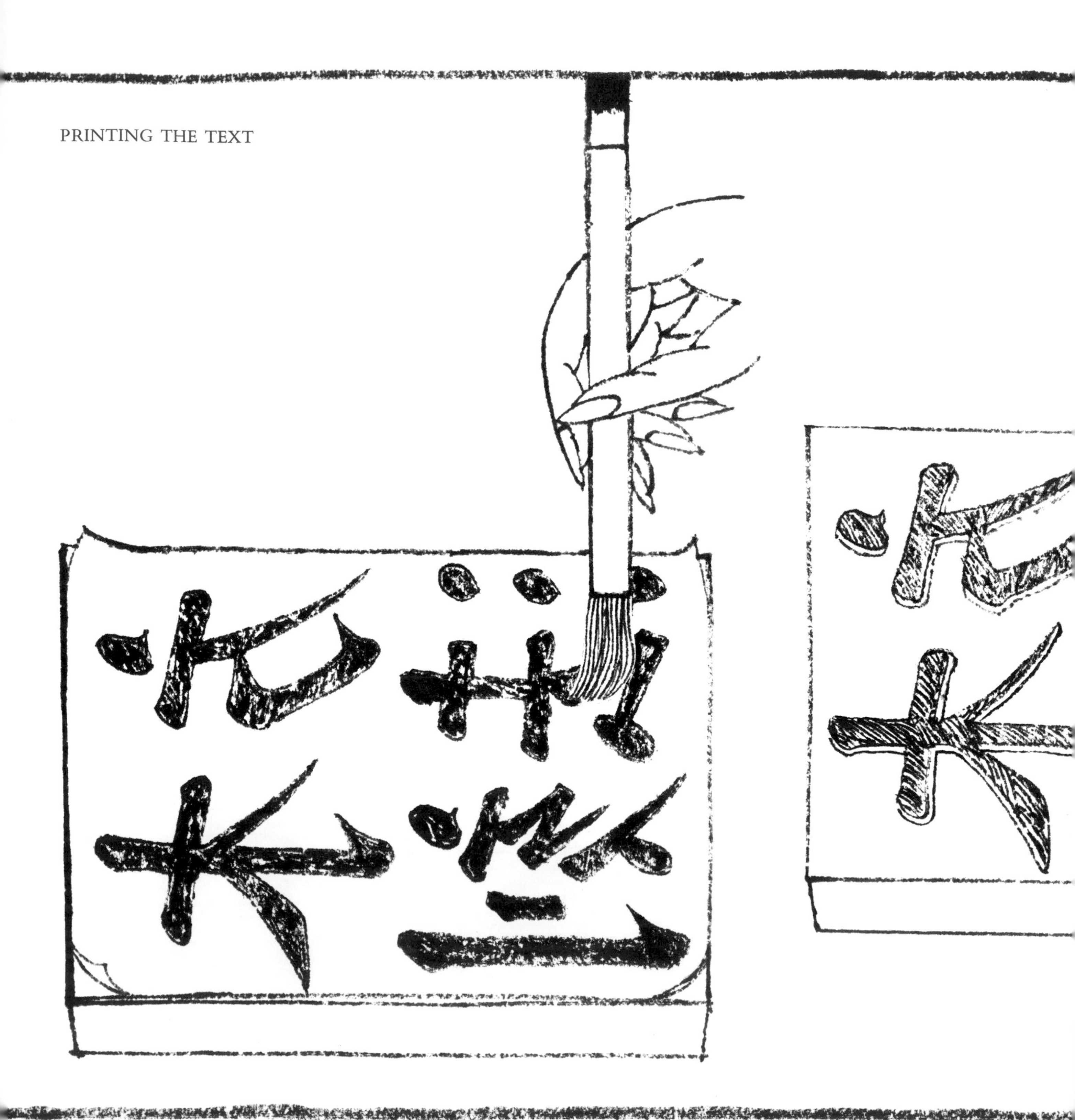

Once the carved block had been inked, the actual printing began. A sheet of paper, made from rags, bark or hemp, was carefully placed on top of the raised characters. Then the printer took the brush that had been used to apply the ink; on the opposite end of the handle there was a dry brush, which the printer ran lightly across the paper (*below, left*). This gentle pressure was sufficient to transfer the characters to the page, which was immediately peeled off the block (*right*) and set aside to dry. Eventually the printed sheets were sewn together in a book. Although the actual printing was completely done by hand, a skilled craftsman could run off as many as 2,000 pages in a single day.

The process, simple as it was, had a lasting impact on Chinese society, as it did later in the West. Books were no longer the privilege of the wealthy, but became a door to education and advancement for anyone who could learn to read.

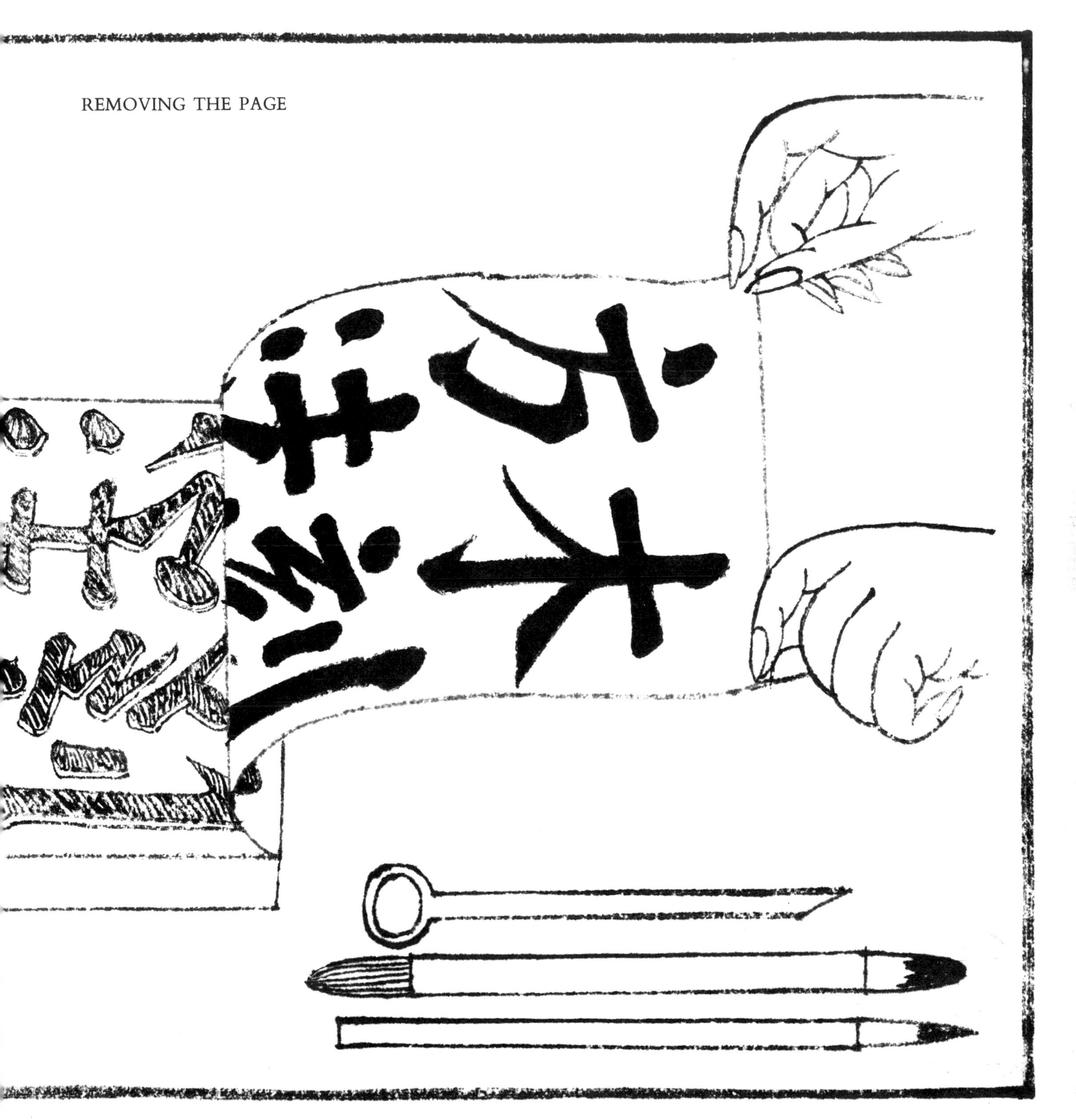

REMOVING THE PAGE

7

A HERITAGE OF WORDS

AN ASSEMBLY OF SCHOLARS, *seen in a detail from a silk scroll painting, was convened by a sixth-century emperor to collate the best in literature for the education of his young son. Familiarity with the great classical texts was an absolute requirement for members of the ruling classes of China.*

The most precious possession of the Chinese people is their language. Through the ages it acquired a vast and flexible vocabulary and grew mature with usage. It is to this language and to the subtle and perceptive men who developed it that Chinese literature owes its greatness.

The classical language—the language in which, until recent times, all literature was written—differs from any of the modern spoken dialects. Basically the characters used in this written language have not changed since the time of Confucius even though the spoken sounds have been greatly modified over the centuries. Thus it is possible for the modern Chinese to read the great works of antiquity—classic histories, venerated documents and several forms of exquisite poetry—pronouncing them as modern Chinese.

Little is known about the speech of the first Hua men. The pictographs that appear on the Shang oracle bones, the earliest known evidence of Chinese writing, give few clues as to how the words representing the objects were pronounced. The language spoken in the classical age—from the seventh to third centuries B.C.—is much less obscure. The sounds of the spoken language of that distant age are now beginning to be learned through advanced linguistic techniques, such as the analysis of rhyme in ancient writings.

From what is known of the pronunciation of Chinese since classical times, it is evident that there has been a constant trend towards simplification, chiefly by the elimination of complex consonant sounds. The speech of Confucius was full of words that might have sounded like *khmad* and *slog*—sounds that would be quite alien to the speech of his modern descendants. "Liu Ch'e", the modern version of the name of the great Han emperor, was "Lyog D'yat" in his own time. By medieval times, Chinese pronunciation was much closer to that of today: Emperor Li Lung-chi and the minister-gardener Li Te-yü called themselves something like Li Lyung-ki and Li Tek-yu.

The phonetic simplification that has gone on since their day is suggested by a list of words used in the written or classical language of medieval times. All are pronounced *hsieh* in the official spoken language of today: *ghai* (apparatus); *ghaai*

THE EVOLUTION OF A CHARACTER *is shown in four drawings. A three-legged pottery jar called a "li" (A) was first represented by a pictograph (B). About 1000* B.C. *the graph resembled bronze vessels of the time (C); since 200* B.C. *it has appeared as in (D).*

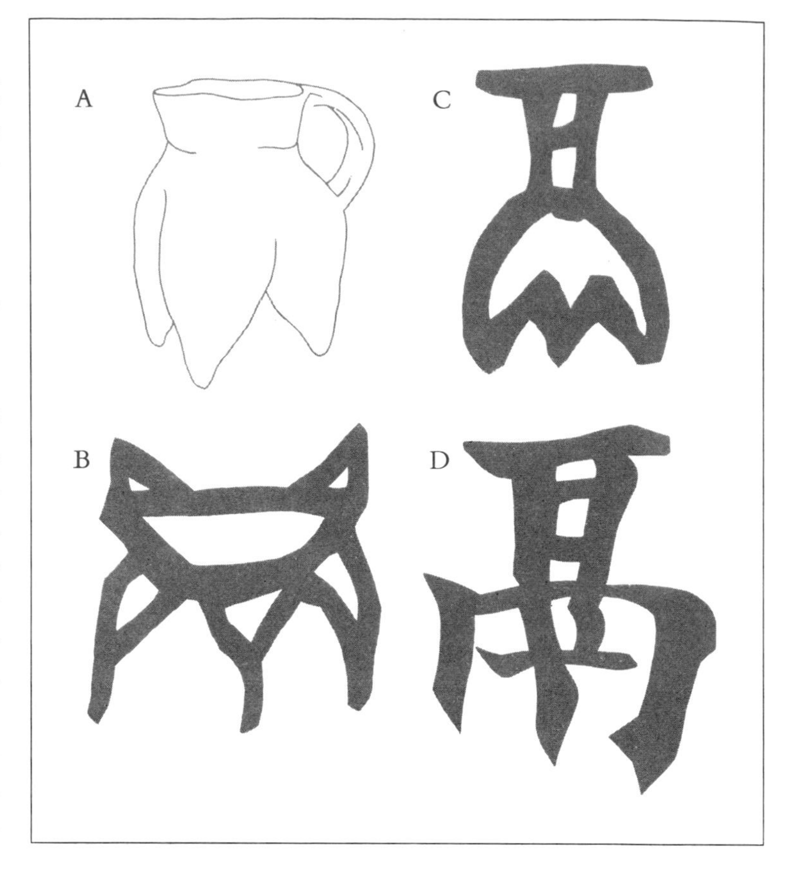

(crab); *ghep* (associate); *ghet* (stiff-necked); *hyap* (rib); *hyat* (pause); *sep* (reconcile); *set* (detritus); *sya* (slight); *syet* (diffuse); *zya* (slant).

Such a radical simplification of sounds might have led to ambiguity if Chinese had remained monosyllabic—one syllable for each word. But modern Chinese is not monosyllabic—most of these old words, if they survive at all, remain only as the syllabic building blocks of longer words of two or more syllables. They have lost their ancient independence and live on, eroded both in sound and in meaning, but retaining their old written symbols. They are now only fragments like our "amphi" (as in amphibian and amphitheatre), "duce" (as in produce and induce) or "tele" (as in telegraph and telephone). Examples are the old word *zya* (slant), which survives as the syllable *hsieh* in such words as *hsieh-tu* (gradient), and the old word *ghep* (associate), which lives on as the syllable *hsieh* in such words as *hsieh-yüeh* (alliance).

Chinese has from the first been written with a unique script which is called logographic. It employs special written symbols, or logograms, each representing a word in the language. It can be compared only to such archaic writing systems as those of the ancient Sumerians, Babylonians and Egyptians, all now long since superseded by simpler and more flexible systems, such as the alphabets used to write English or Greek.

The earliest of the logograms were apparently pictographic. In the inscriptions on the Shang oracle bones, the sign for the word meaning "horse" is recognizable as a drawing of the animal. We can hardly detect this origin, however, in the cursive form for horse that has been used since the late classical age, when it became simply an arbitrary sign for the word.

A later variation on the logogram that found its way into the written language is the rebus. A rebus is a pictograph that has been borrowed to represent another word sounding exactly like the first one—as in childhood games with English sentences that use the picture of an eye to represent "I", or the picture of a saw to represent the past tense of "see". It takes time to memorize such a script, but, once learned, it is hard to forget. The little patterns of lines soon become indelible mental images of the words they represent.

The contributions of the peculiar script to the continuity and unity of Chinese culture may indeed outweigh its disadvantages in flexibility. The sign for what is now called "Lo", the name of the historic river, was read as "Glak" by Confucius and as "Lak" by the early T'ang rulers, but the symbol for the name of the river has not changed. The script remains intelligible to speakers of extremely varying dialects: people who cannot understand one another's speech can read one another's writing, and all can read the same literature. In contrast, European script is based on the analysis of sounds, and written material can be understood only if the spoken language is understood. If Europeans wrote the word for man, for example, as a stylized stick figure, as the Chinese do, the French could read it as *"homme"*, the Spanish as *"hombre"* and the Italians as *"uomo"*.

The vocabulary of classical Chinese, the old bookman's language, began to expand very early. More conservative than the colloquial language, it retained many words that had been culled from ancient texts and that would otherwise have been obsolete. By Han times, the classical scribes were founding a great lexicographical tradition, recording linguistic oddities from strange parts of the land, and these words too found their way into the classical language.

The glosses and comments that generations of scholars had made on the classics—poems, treatises, histories—which were preserved along with the classics, constituted another rich treasury of words and images for the imaginative use of literate men. Thus, clinging on to the old while admitting the new, classical Chinese developed an enormous and diversified vocabulary in which the most refined distinctions of meaning and the most subtle variations in colour, tone and feeling could be expressed.

The Chinese style of calligraphy changed gradually as new techniques were developed. Until about the second century B.C., Chinese writing was usually incised on hard surfaces. The inscriptions on the bones and shells of the Shang oracle archives were followed by those cast on the surfaces of the ritual bronzes of Shang and Chou. Characters incised on narrow slips of wood or bamboo that were bound up with thongs were the usual scrolls of the age of Confucius. By Han times, the brush came into use and characters were written in carbon-black ink on silk scrolls.

By the second century A.D., after paper had been invented, scrolls were made by gluing sheets of paper together, end to end, in imitation of the silk scrolls. The paper scroll then became the standard book during the age of division and the early medieval period. The Court calligraphers of T'ang, copying from carefully collated texts, made uniform versions of all kinds of instructive books. They used the finest papers from the palace factory, tinted delicately in lemon-yellow, sulphur-yellow or slate-blue, then rolled it on cylinders of ivory or sandalwood that were tipped with knobs of jade, amber or rock crystal.

In the ninth century, Buddhist texts began to appear in a new form: accordion-folded manuscripts. By the next century, such manuscripts were not only folded but also stitched along the edge of one set of folds to make real books.

As a result of the invention of block printing, the making of scrolls and books was greatly facilitated. At first, printed matter was limited primarily to Buddhist and Taoist religious tracts; later the government took advantage of the printing process to disseminate the Confucian classics. By late medieval times, books were printed on one side of separate sheets of very thin paper, two pages per sheet. Each sheet was then folded in the centre so that the printed side remained outside and the blank sides were back to back. In the finished book the folds were at the right, as in the accordion-folded manuscript, and the cut edges were stitched together. This process made possible wide dissemination of historical, literary and religious works.

By medieval times, China was on its way to becoming a kingdom of books, and the literary profession held high status. But this climb had been a slow process for the pioneering men of letters, who at first were only minor palace employees.

The poets of early times had been honoured for their linguistic artistry, primarily when they used it to glorify the Son of Heaven and the world of which he approved. They were required to produce formal odes, eulogies and paeans; poems that did not fit these patterns might be suppressed or heavily edited. As late as mid-Han times, as Wang Ch'ung reports, the best hope of literary men had been employment as collators in the office of the royal astrologer or of the royal liturgist.

After the fall of the Han Dynasty, the number of poems not devoted to the glorification of the monarchy increased wonderfully, but some of the old censorious attitude remained. In A.D. 833, the T'ang emperor, a well-bred, literate, musical young man, proposed to establish a new academic degree to be called "Gentlemen Learned in Poetry". His adviser dissuaded him: "The poets of today are superficial and paltry—in nothing gainful to good order", he told the emperor. The adviser's opinion was behind the times. Some of the greatest of Chinese poets were writing then, and the impractical professors and poetic dreamers were generally being accorded recognition.

The ranks of learned men had been greatly expanded in the early medieval period by the system of government examinations that made it possible for men from outside the aristocracy—even for some not born in the old Middle Kingdom—to hold high office and thus be accepted into the *élite*. To pass the examinations and make their way into high positions, the candidates had to be familiar with the classical books—religious, ceremonial and political—and their orthodox interpretations. This small body of texts was regarded as the basis of all civilized life, and an important part of literary composition consisted of writing interpretations of the canons or works influenced by them.

Some of the texts that the cultured T'ang gentlemen had to become familiar with have survived. A few contain fragments of writings that, though written as early as the ninth or tenth century B.C., exhibit real literary merit.

Most revered were the purported histories of ancient times. Among these are parts of a mixed collection, the *Shu Ching*, "Canon of Writings", which

THE OLDEST CHINESE TEXT *done on silk shows a calendar naming each month—as well as astronomical signs and paintings of trees and antlered gods. The silk manuscript dates from around 500* B.C.

is commonly known in the West as the "Classic of History". Orthodox critics in China long regarded these texts as the actual decrees and pronouncements of early Chou kings, but modern scholarship has disclosed that the accounts are not historical but legendary and ritualistic. They are probably thoroughly revised libretti for archaic religious dramas —similar to the miracle plays of medieval Europe— in which actors represented deified kings or humanized gods of the glorious past.

Other hallowed classics of varying content and age included dull chronicles, exciting anecdotes, models of noble behaviour and primitive divination lore. In the interpretation accepted by the medieval Chinese, these works were revelations of the vanished world of Confucius and his forerunners. The picture they gave was honourable but doubtful, as the Greece of Pericles and Plato was revealed to the men of the Renaissance, full of wonder and glory, but in many respects a fairy-tale world.

The oldest canonical history books were the annals called "Springs and Autumns". These were hallowed in the belief—probably unfounded—that they had been compiled and annotated by Confucius, and they were accepted as classics of Chou scholarship despite their threadbare, primitive style.

But historiography was one of the great arts of the Chinese and the medieval student also had access to some excellent documents in that field. Among these were the so-called "Dynastic Histories", whose chief flaw was the partiality they showed for persons and ideas favoured in official Confucian circles. The first such history was written by Szu-ma Ch'ien, a genius of the second century B.C. who had been a palace scribe at the Court of Emperor Liu Ch'e. His pioneering work was the prototype of many succeeding dynastic histories, which were increasingly subject to official control and the pressure of courtiers and Court lobbies.

Related to the histories were the anthologies

of "administrative prose"—memorials, manifestos, edicts, addresses, memoranda, petitions—which were read not only as examples of meritorious intellectual and practical compositions but for their literary value. These held an honoured position in Chinese literature quite different from the status of most such documents in European culture.

Like other classics, these administrative documents were emulated by the practising medieval writers, sometimes in works dealing with bizarre themes. Han Yü, the very paragon of the official T'ang writer, composed a memorial to the throne on the subject of government preparations to receive a religious relic—one of the Buddha's bones. Though widely admired for its literary quality, it still offended many important people by its tactless attack on a sacred belief. Equally famous was Han Yü's fulmination against the crocodiles of Ch'ao-chou, written as an official address to the reptiles in his role as priestly magistrate.

Important changes in the ancient traditions in literature developed in the age of division, between the third and seventh centuries A.D., when new ways of treating nature began to appear. These were partly inspired by Taoist and Buddhist tenets and by the natural beauty of the subtropical south, which was settled at this time by intellectuals escaping the unrest in the north.

Liu Tsung-yüan, a protégé of Han Yü who was in exile in the far south, was the first writer of outstanding talent to use the exotic scenery there as his theme. His description of a high peak near his place of banishment began:

> *This mountain rises in a knotted cluster in the midst of blurred blue. Galloping clouds, running straight up and reaching out ten thousands of miles, coil round this wild retreat. From its head pour great torrents, and all the other hills come to attend its levee—their aspect like that of stars showing reverence [to the pole star], in deceptive images of grey-green and halcyon-blue, strung in damask designs, interlaced in embroideries. Indeed it appears that Heaven has assembled its choicest blooms in this place. . . .*

Other types of prose that survive from T'ang times are fables, fairy tales and romances, indications of uneasiness with rigid Confucian orthodoxy, that often reveal the other-worldly influence of Taoism. They related things somehow believable and incredible at the same time. Telling of travel backwards in time, of visits to improbable ghostly worlds, and of the splendours and wonders of distant places, they played the same role in medieval Chinese life that science fiction does in our own.

Despite the excellence and variety of Chinese prose, it is Chinese poetry that has had the greatest world-wide appeal. The oldest surviving Chinese poetry, some of it dating from the tenth or ninth century B.C., is found in another "Confucian" classic, the *Shih Ching*, known as the "Book of Odes". This is a medley of ritual hymns, paeans to great war-lords, wedding chants and folk poetry—altered over the centuries, no doubt, by critics and Court poets. All this poetry, whether secular or ritual, had been, by T'ang times, forced into the mould of Confucian morality to serve as pious lessons to the Chinese students. These lessons would probably have bewildered the ancient poets, who wrote their verses to celebrate the mysteries of antiquity, the excitement of courtship or the glory of famous princes. But they had become models for medieval poets, and few writers failed to learn these archaic and sometimes badly interpreted lyrics by heart and to echo them in their own works.

A similar destiny awaited the ancient collection of poetry now called the *Ch'u Tz'u*—a mass of fervent, ecstatic, sometimes extravagant verse that comes down to us, for the most part from the end of the Chou period, as an extraordinary example of beautiful writing, entirely alien to the so-called classic tradition. The *Ch'u Tz'u* poems were mainly celebrations of the voyage of the soul to supernatural worlds, guide-books to unseen paradises and projections of shamanistic fancy. But the anthology was accepted as a kind of minor classic, after it had been adapted to majority belief by scores of official editors and interpreters. By Han times, many of the *Ch'u Tz'u* poems were interpreted as political satires and guides to ethics.

The words of these classics became the building blocks for later poetry and fortunately some poets knew how to use them well. Their form was also followed in medieval times: from the *Shih Ching* came the symmetrical lyric, or *shih*, and from the *Ch'u Tz'u* the descriptive rhapsody, or *fu*.

The ancient *shih* followed a distinct rhythmic form: the lines were rhymed couplets composed of four, five or seven words each. After Han times another peculiarity was added to this basic structure—the words in every line had their parallels in the following line. In the example that follows, "evening" and "spring", both words for natural time periods, are paralleled in sense and function. "River" matches "flowers", "flat" goes with "full", "not" with "just", "moving" with "opened", and so on, pair by pair:

Evening river—flat, not moving:
Spring flowers—full, just opened.
Drifting waves go off, carrying moon,
Tidal waves come in—girded with stars.

The poem, which rhymes in the original Chinese, is a vision of the mouth of the river Yangtze, seen under the full moon, with the ocean tide rising, just as the stars begin to appear in the darkening east.

Though the *shih* continued to be influenced by ancient models, it was also constantly being refreshed by folk-poetry and popular songs. It revealed a personal and intimate view of the world—internal and intense.

The *fu*, a less symmetrical form of poetry than the *shih*, was usually devoted to a single topic, which it celebrated in the most florid and rich vocabulary possible. Though the form was applied to such subjects as elephants, walled cities and the textile industry, the poem was seldom prosaic. This is illustrated in the following lines by the seventh-century poet Ts'ui Tun-li in which he tells why he planted pine seedlings in the mountains:

There are trees, which, having luxuriated quickly, are the first to topple,
And there are creatures which, having proliferated speedily, are suddenly worn out.
We set out peach and plum to flower early;
We plant elm and willow for easy shade;
The Mongol Oak, split for faggots, thrives all the more;
The Tree of Heaven, pruned for fuel, comes back to life.
But all of these
Will break and snap, as aftermath of flying snow—
Will be consumed to the heart by a spell of severe frost.
Take the pine on the other hand:
Its trunk resists wind and thunder,
Its roots split cliff and rock . . .
How then indeed can such as this be compared with the mediocre stock of the mass of trees?

The *fu* tended to become a virtuoso piece, offered by a Court poet on imperial command, to celebrate some splendid event. Detached from its emotional and mystical origins, the *fu* became more and more a courtly verbal game. The style was never given up, though few of the later writers ever handled it as well as the earliest masters had.

A third poetic form was the *tz'u*, a product of

the decaying society of the late T'ang. It was based on the popular songs—many of which were pseudo-exotic or of foreign origin—sung by female entertainers in the cafés of the capital city. Dazzled young *littérateurs* learned to sing these songs, memorized the tunes and set new words to them.

Verses in this new form of poetry tended to be romantic, nostalgic, bitter-sweet:

The place I saw her—
A late evening sky—
Under the thorny t'ung in front of the Terrace of Viet;
In the darkness, turning pupils deeply fixed with meaning,
She dropped a pair of kingfisher ornaments,
Mounted on elephant, turned her back on me —went ahead over the water.

Regardless of form, Chinese poetry tended to reflect those themes that were of paramount importance to the people: personal relationships, nostalgia for the past and reverence for nature.

The greatest theme of Chinese poetry was human relationships. The love of friends, of spouse, of children—often the unhappy side of personal attachments—is a recurrent theme. Sad poems about partings, loneliness, homesickness, journeys in strange places and cruel environments numbered in the thousands. They demonstrate why the ancient punishment of exile was regarded as so severe. A poem from the brush of the T'ang poet Ts'en Shen, a man familiar with life in provincial military headquarters and harsh garrisons, tells of the feelings of Chinese guests at a party in the town of Wine Springs on the Central Asian frontier:

The Grand Protector of Wine Springs, expert at the sword dance,
Set out the wine in his high hall—his drums beat in the night.
Just one song on the barbarian pipe rent our bowels—
We seated visitors gazed at each other, our tears like rain.

Love of friends and family is a more popular theme in Chinese poetry than romantic love, but, despite a widespread notion to the contrary, Chinese poets did write about their feelings for women. As time went on, they expressed themselves quite directly and emotionally—sometimes even sensually. This was especially true in the late T'ang period, an age when a number of great writers were known for their complicated love affairs. From this same period there are even love poems written by women—Court ladies, Taoist "nuns" and, especially, courtesans.

The transience of life and the evanescence of all human attachments, the second most popular theme of Chinese poetry, was closely related to the first. It permitted nostalgia for the past, and a kind of reminiscent romanticism became as popular a theme with early medieval Chinese poets as romantic love has been with Western poets.

These dreams of the wonderful times of old supplied Chinese writers with colourful images—all too often stereotypes and *clichés*—for the embroidery of their verses. For every Daphnis and Chloë, every Caesar and Brutus available to the European poet, there were counterparts in Chinese tradition, to be alluded to in a thousand intricate ways. All personages and events recorded in historical books or living in oral legend were subjects for literary allusion. The poets foraged these rich fields voraciously.

The melancholy that had infected the poems of antiquity became intensified during the declining decades of T'ang, when all beautiful things seemed illusory, all human values decaying. This attitude was reinforced by the Buddhist concept of the vanity of appearances in the light of eternity. Both are exemplified in a poem by Szu-K'ung Shu, written in the eighth century, about an abandoned monastery in Ch'ang-an:

> *By the yellow leaves—a temple from an earlier reign;*
> *No monks are there—the cold basilica stands open.*
> *Where the pool shows fair, a turtle comes out and suns itself;*
> *Where the pines make a shade, a crane flies out and around.*
> *On old flagstones, the steles are crossed with grass;*
> *In shadowed galleries, the pictures are patched with moss.*
> *Even the Palace of Contemplation is spent and melted away—*
> *This world of dust still wants more of our grief.*

The third great theme of Chinese poetry was nature and it was seldom absent, even in poems emphasizing other moods. In the very oldest verses, nature is portrayed chiefly as the medium through which the purposes of the gods—benevolent or terrifying—are made clear. This treatment of the natural world survived for centuries in good conservative contexts—ritual pronouncements, prayers and panegyrics, royal eulogies. Out of this kind of symbolism came the common attitude of the classical age that nature and living things are only worth noticing as symbols of ideas and emotions. Writers used nature to set the mood or tone of a poem or exploited it in complex allegories.

After the migration of the gentry southwards during the barbarian occupation of the northlands, literate intellectuals began to regard nature as a fit topic in its own right. The verbal resources of the old urban, practical, political past began to be transmuted into a language suitable to this fresher,

HIGHLIGHTS OF LITERATURE

Literary landmarks and noted authors of ancient China are listed below. The first five works, of unknown authorship, are called "Confucian Classics" because the sage supposedly taught them. The next three from the Chou period are mystical and philosophical. Histories and fu poetry, a flowery, irregular verse form, were the pride of Han times. Later authors favoured shih poetry, a more measured lyric.

CHOU DYNASTY 1000–221 B.C.	*Book of Changes (I Ching)*	
	Book of History (Shu Ching)	
	Book of Odes (Shih Ching)	
	Spring and Autumn Annals	
	Record of Rites (Li Chi)	
	Confucian Analects	
	The Meng Tzu	MENCIUS (372–289 B.C.)
	The Ch'u Tz'u	
HAN DYNASTY 206 B.C.–A.D. 220	*Fu* Poetry	SZU-MA HSIANG-JU (179–117 B.C.) YANG HSIUNG (53 B.C.–A.D. 18) PAN KU (A.D. 32–92) CHANG HENG (A.D. 78–139)
	The Records of the Historian (Shih-chi)	SZU-MA CH'IEN (145–86 B.C.)
	The History of the Former Han (Han-shu)	PAN KU (A.D. 32–92)
	Lun Heng	WANG CH'UNG (A.D. 27–97)
THREE KINGDOMS A.D. 220–265	*Shih* Poetry	TS'AO CHIH (A.D. 192–232)
NORTHERN AND SOUTHERN DYNASTIES A.D. 316–589	*Shih* Poetry	T'AO CH'IEN (A.D. 365–427)
	Wen Hsüan	HSIAO T'UNG (A.D. 501–531)
T'ANG DYNASTY A.D. 618–907	*Shih* Poetry	WANG WEI (A.D. 699–759) LI PO (A.D. 701–762) TU FU (A.D. 712–770) PO CHÜ-I (A.D. 772–846) LI HO (A.D. 790–816) LI SHANG-YIN (A.D. 812–858)
	Neo-Classical Prose	HAN YÜ (A.D. 768–824) LIU TSUNG-YÜAN (A.D. 773–819)
	Stories and Tales	PO HSING-CHIEN (d. A.D. 826)
	Buddhist Tales	
	Tzu Poetry	

lovelier world. A new kind of nature poetry came into being along with the new age of gardens. Nevertheless, the new natural world was never entirely divested of its supernatural significance; down into medieval times, Chinese poetry continued to represent the glories of nature as semblances of the divine world.

The best lyrics written during the age of division adopt this mystical view of existence. They show nature not as a pretty environment for the recreation of aristocrats, nor as the barren retreat of idlers, nor as the ominous world interpreted by diviners and medicine-men—although all these ways of looking at nature remained alive. Rather, the best post-classical writers saw the non-urban landscape as a physical model or foretaste of paradise and its infinite suburbs. Walking in meadow and forest, they were inspired to anticipate free-and-easy wandering beyond the high seas and among the stars. Refreshing themselves under the trees, they contemplated the transcendental life promised by Taoism.

Literature expressing this great hope was a protest against the unstable and often bloody life of an era when uncouth nomads were planting alfalfa for their herds where once there had been fields of maize, millet and barley, when the tame acceptance of brutality and irreverence might, it seemed, come to dominate Chinese life. Nature offered both escape and a new kind of design.

The presence of the divine world persisted, however faintly, in some post-classical Chinese poetry, although it was essentially a secular art. Taoist and Buddhist ideas, usually subdued or disguised, are common in the literature of the T'ang period, when both Taoist and Buddhist other-worldliness was accepted by much of established society as a possible way of understanding man's destiny. But the tendency to express supernatural longing by symbolism, allusiveness and indirection encouraged superficiality—a sliding away from sincerity into mere elegance and polish. Some "Taoist" poems of the T'ang period were mainly devices for giving acceptable form to erotic dreams of slender, white-armed nymphs in flowered palace courtyards. So Taoist poetry came to resemble Court poetry.

All Chinese poetry, whatever the form and whatever the theme, sought to instruct, to improve, to liberate. But the straightforward didactic poetry so familiar in the West was not in the Chinese style; multiple meanings and indirect references were preferred. Chinese poets hoped to express, through the magic of words, their feelings about the problems of ordinary living, the delights of the imagination, and the passionate longing of man for truth—all at one time.

The spread of the Chinese language—and hence of the influence of Chinese literature—coincided with the spread of Chinese political dominance. The neighbours immediately south of the old Middle Kingdom speaking monosyllabic languages related to Chinese, were easy to absorb. The southern expansion did not stop until it reached the border of Champa, where people spoke a Malayan language. The neighbours immediately north, ancestors of the modern Turks, Mongols and Manchus, spoke polysyllabic languages and absorbed little of the Chinese language or the Chinese civilization.

The Japanese, the Koreans and the Vietnamese never adopted the Chinese language, but, as their culture expanded in medieval times, they began to draw heavily on the treasury of Chinese words and Chinese thought. The Vietnamese—and even some speakers of polysyllabic languages—also adapted the Chinese script. To them the language and literature of classical China were what those of classical Greece and Rome have been to Europe and those of Arabia to the Near East—an inexhaustible well of words and ideas.

THE POETRY OF THE LAND

Each time that I look at a fine landscape:
I raise my voice and recite a stanza of poetry.

The ninth-century Chinese poet Po Chü-i, who wrote these lines, might have been speaking for Chinese poets through the ages. Nowhere have men been so inspired by the grandeur of their native land; nowhere has the land so perfectly lent itself to poetic description. In the mountains of China's south-west, tumultuous rivers race through deep gorges. Along the Pacific coast, slower, wider rivers meander through a broad delta where placid lakes yield a rich harvest of fish. In the drier country to the north, fields of grain terrace steep hill-sides. Lying across China's northern borders is the Gobi Desert, a bone-dry wasteland, and beyond it stretch the grey and dusty plains of the Mongolian steppes. The splendour of this variegated terrain has stimulated Chinese poets so powerfully that the description of landscape is a nearly universal element in Chinese poetry. It is the theme of the simple, graceful lines written by Po Chü-i in the ninth century A.D. and of the verse of Szu-ma Hsiang-ju in the second century B.C., poets who evoke curiously timeless landscapes. The photographs on these pages were taken in this century; the poetry that accompanies them was written before the tenth century A.D., yet is as apt today as it was then—and as it undoubtedly will be 1,000 years from now.

LAKE LI-HU, YANGTZE RIVER DELTA

from "Chu-ch'en Village"

The girls go drawing the water from the brook;
The men go gathering fire-wood on the hill . . .
Alive, they are the people of Ch'en Village;
Dead, they become the dust of Ch'en Village.

PO CHÜ-I, NINTH CENTURY A.D.

VILLAGE ON THE RIVER YANGTZE, CENTRAL CHINA

"Duckweed Pond"

By the spring pond, deep and wide,
You must be waiting for the light boat to return.
Supple and soft, the green duckweed meshes,
Till dangling willows sweep it open again.

WANG WEI, EIGHT CENTURY A.D.

WEST LAKE, OFF THE RIVER HUAI
EASTERN CHINA

from "Cold Mountain"

In winding valleys too tortuous to trace,
On crags piled who knows how high,
A thousand different grasses weep with dew
And pines hum together in the wind.

HAN-SHAN, EIGHT OR NINTH CENTURY A.D.

VALLEY IN SZECHWAN, WESTERN CHINA

RIVER YANGTZE GORGE, SZECHWAN, WESTERN CHINA

from "Fu on the Yangtze"

In the gorges east of Pa,
Where the Lord of Hsia chiselled a path for the waters,
Broken cliffs plunge ten thousand feet,
Their wall-like faces ragged in mist;
The lone peak of Tiger Tooth soars to the sky,
And the Gate of Ching rises, towering and majestic.
There the curve-bound pools spin nine times round, swelling and subsiding,
And the fierce currents roar like thunder, dart with lightning's speed.

KUO PU, THIRD CENTURY A.D.

"Peasant Song"

At sunrise to work,
Sunset to rest,
Drinking from a well I dug,
Eating off the fields I plough—
The Emperor and his might—what are they to me?

ANONYMOUS

TERRACED HILL-SIDE, WESTERN BORDERLAND

from
"Planting Bamboos"

I planted bamboos,
more than a
hundred shoots.
When I see their
beauty, as they grow
by the stream-side,
I feel again as though
I lived in the hills,
And many a time on
public holidays
Round their railing I
walk till night comes

PO CHÜ-I, NINTH CENTURY A.D.

BAMBOO GROVE, EASTERN CHINA

RIVER FUCHUN

from "Written Aboard a Boat"

A boat on the Spring waters–Like sitting on top of the sky.

TU FU, EIGHTH CENTURY A.D.

from "Fu on the Shang-lin Park"

The steep summits of the Nine Pikes,
The towering heights of the Southern Mountains,
Soar dizzily like a stack of cooking pots,
Precipitous and sheer.

SZU-MA HSIANG-JU, SECOND CENTURY B.C.

MOUNTAIN RANGE, SOUTHERN COAST

8

CHINA AND THE OUTER WORLD

FOUNDER OF A GOLDEN AGE, *the Emperor T'ai Tsung overthrew the Sui Dynasty in A.D. 618, subjugated surrounding peoples and conquered large tracts of Central Asia, initiating the 300-year rule of the T'ang Dynasty.*

China taught the world and China learned from it. Through the centuries China's influence on its neighbours—particularly Japan, Korea and Tibet—was incalculable, and its contributions to world civilization ranged from mechanical clocks and fireworks to porcelain and poetry. In turn it owed much of its own richness and diversity in medieval times to fruitful connections with other cultures.

These connections came about through imperial conquest and trade, and even through religion. The territory controlled by China expanded from the little Middle Kingdom in the Yellow river valley, which was the Chinese world to the feudal baron Szu-ma Niu in the fifth century B.C., to the vast domains reaching out north-west and south, which were controlled by the great Emperor Li Lung-chi at the height of T'ang power. Traders followed in the footsteps of the conquering soldiers and later reached out far beyond the Chinese world. Zealous pilgrims roamed through all Asia in search of Buddhist shrines and brought back with them the riches of neighbouring lands. And finally, more distant influences were brought by adventurous foreigners who came from as far as Persia and Byzantium to enjoy the splendours of medieval China.

How much of China's earliest culture resulted from contact with other ancient civilizations is still a tantalizing question. A century or so ago it was believed that no significant element of Chinese culture—the religion, cosmology, writing system—could have developed entirely within China itself. All the basic ideas must have come, it was thought, from Mesopotamia, or Egypt, or some other cradle of civilization better known to the West. There are few people today who accept this as the complete story, though it is difficult to filter any truly reliable information from the meagre and ambiguous data provided by ancient Chinese sources. One thing is clear, however—ideas and goods flowed both in and out of China from the earliest times.

It is known, for instance, that contacts between the ancient Hua men and other peoples in remote antiquity were motivated primarily by the need for items used in religious rituals. The oldest Chinese records show that among the most important of the goods brought in from other countries were pigments required for ceremonial purposes—for painting temples, altars, the bodies of celebrants and ritual objects of all kinds. Jade, the holy gemstone, had always come from some 1,500 miles away in Central Asia.

The earliest intimations of the existence of foreign trade reveal not only the religious motives of the traders but also the spiritual aura of their mission. The traveller had to prepare himself for encounters with the many spirits, good and bad, that lurked beyond the frontiers of the Middle Kingdom. There were baleful demons to be appeased and strange gods to be adored. Part of the role of guide-books in Ancient China was to acquaint the far wanderer with the supernatural problems of his journey. Indeed, in the Bronze Age there could have been little to distinguish the worldly peregrinations of a slave trader's trembling body from the cosmic explorations of a shaman's shivering soul.

After the fall of the Chou Dynasty in the third century B.C. the Chinese world expanded rapidly. Under the Ch'in and Han Dynasties, foreign contacts multiplied—and were better documented—as China began to absorb old neighbours by force and thus encountered new ones.

To the north of the Middle Kingdom there was a confederacy of nomadic tribes called the Hsiung-nu, and protecting the frontier against these barbarians had always been important to the Hua men. At this time it became doubly important to contain the Hsiung-nu in order to establish control over the lucrative trade routes to the West. This was done both by war and by intrigue.

Chinese expansion in the north-west began with a diplomatic mission arranged by the powerful Han emperor, Liu Ch'e. It came about because he and his advisers feared the power of the Hsiung-nu, who at that time had overcome another great nomadic tribe, the Yüeh-chih, and made the skull of its king into a wine goblet. The defeated tribe had driven its flocks far into the west and Liu Ch'e decided to find it and propose an alliance.

The emperor's chief purpose was to weaken the Hsiung-nu, and he hoped to play on the desire of the defeated Yüeh-chih to avenge the ignominious death of their king and thus to restore their national honour. The man Liu Ch'e chose for an emissary was a courtier named Chang Ch'ien. He was the right man for the job—a robust, big-hearted fellow who treated all men fairly, whatever their race, and who was quick to make friends in strange nations. He now ranks among the greatest of explorers and travellers, comparable only to men like Marco Polo and Magellan.

At first Chang Ch'ien's great mission seemed unlikely to succeed. He was captured by the Hsiung-nu on his way through the deadly salt deserts and grassy wastes into Central Asia, and spent many years among them. He took a native wife, who bore him children. But he never forgot his important errand. He escaped from the Hsiung-nu encampment and continued on his way west accompanied by a native guide. He is the first Chinese known to have visited the Iranian nations of Ferghana, Samarkand and Bactria. Eventually he found the Hsiung-nu enemies, but they had by then established a new and fertile base on the north-west frontier of India and were content to remain aloof from Far Eastern intrigue.

The great Han empire was literally founded in Chang Ch'ien's footsteps. When this explorer-diplomat returned and reported on the riches he had seen, the Han armies marched. They took control of the route west and extended the confines of the empire as far as Sogdiana.

Chang Ch'ien's discoveries also influenced life at home. The horses of the new Chinese cavalry grazed on the fields of alfalfa grown from the seeds he brought back; the aristocracy ate the grapes that

A FAREWELL SCENE *set against a background of Mongol tents, saddled horses and camels—illustrates a famous Chinese story. It shows Wen-chi, a captive Chinese wife ransomed after 12 years in the north, taking leave of her Mongol husband. (He is the heavy, dark-robed figure standing with her on the right, his sleeves raised to his face to hide his grief.) During China's era of expansion northwestwards, many women like Wen-chi were married off to—or carried off by—such northern chieftains.*

his explorations brought to their tables for the first time. In later times, so great was his fame as an introducer of new plants that almost any novelty introduced into the gardens and orchards of the Chinese was confidently attributed to the diligence of Chang Ch'ien.

The route to the West that had been pioneered by Chang Ch'ien was reopened in medieval times. The workshops of the T'ang palace required alum from Qočo in Central Asia for glazing fine paper, and jade from Khotan for making ornaments and sacred objects. Court goldsmiths could not solder the metals they worked with without ammonium chloride from the volcanic fumaroles in Central Asia or the borax from the dry desert lakes in Tibet.

To keep these routes open the Chinese had to hold the frontier against the ever-threatening barbarians. This was often accomplished without the necessity of going to war by appeasing the pastoral nomads with gifts of Chinese silk, wine and women. Indeed the diplomatic marriage was to become a very important element of Chinese policy. A fur-hatted northern chieftain was almost certain to be delighted by the proffering of an aristocratic Chinese girl as a wife, although the pale-skinned, fastidious young lady involved in the transaction might not be so happy with her new life, which had to be spent in a felt tent that stank with boiled mutton and fermented milk. An old poem reflects the feelings of such a delicate exile:

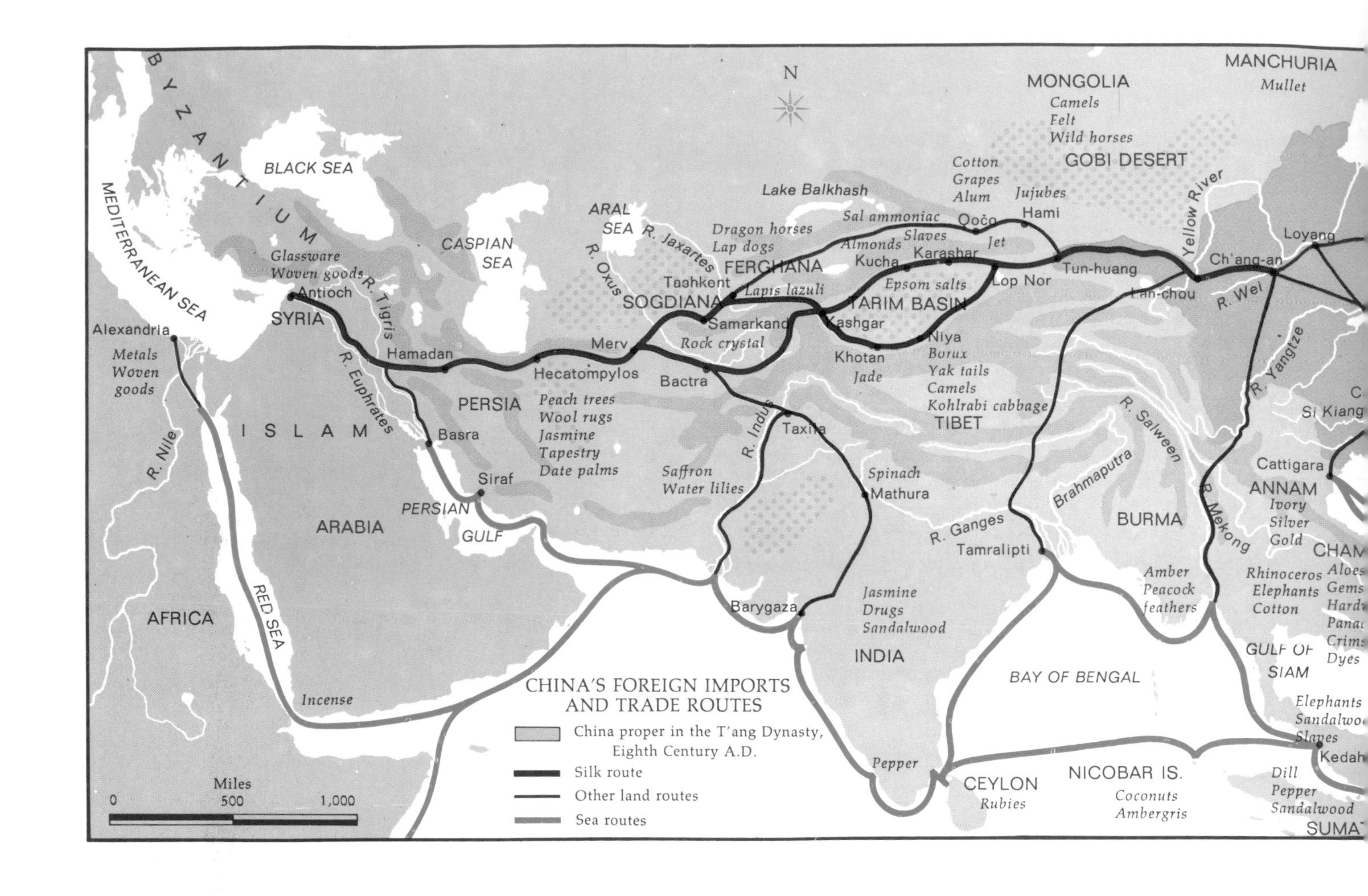

My household married me off—Oh!
under another sky,
Gave me in custody, in a strange land—Oh!
to the king of the Wu-sun.
A vaulted hut for a house—Oh!
with felt for wall,
I use flesh for food—Oh!
koumiss for liqueur.
Thoughts of my own soil are always with me—Oh!
wounded deep in my heart
I could wish to be a yellow swan—Oh!
to return to my old home—

At the same time as the Chinese began to expand vigorously to the north-west, they also turned in the direction in which lay their true destiny—the south. The armies of Ch'in and Han extended the southern border of their land beyond the river Yangtze into country barely conceived of by men of the Bronze Age. They pushed through the great virgin forests of the monsoon lands, beyond the Tropic of Cancer, to the thunderous coast of the South China Sea. Then their emperor declared that these lands, populated by head-hunters and crocodiles, were also Chinese lands.

The First Emperor of Ch'in created three huge provinces, with hazy boundaries, on the South Sea coast and named them "South Sea", "Cinnamon Forest" and "Elephant". The central government was unable to retain its hold over this vast and distant tropical wilderness, however, and it was soon taken over by a Chinese war-lord Chao T'o, who declared himself King of Nam-Viet, extended his kingdom into the area that was to become North Vietnam and ruled it all from a base near modern Canton. He eventually bequeathed this

A NETWORK OF TRADE ROUTES *by land and sea linked China to the outer world during T'ang times. Over roads like the Silk Route, which skirted mountains and deserts, China exported her famous silk and imported luxury goods. Among these imports, many of them previously unknown to the Chinese, were almonds from Kucha, peach trees from Persia and glassware from Syria.*

strange realm to the Han emperors, but they had little better success than their predecessors in holding on to the south-coastal possessions.

In the first century A.D., however, a septuagenarian war-lord, Ma Yüan, "Wave Tamer", reclaimed the territory and finally made the Hua men the true masters of the tropical coast. Ma Yüan established his name for ever in local folk-lore as a great admiral and general who erected two bronze pillars at the new southern limits of the civilized world, beyond which were only demons, ghosts and sub-human savages. But the world beyond the pillars was also the source of magic night-shining pearls, drugs of unheard of potency and incenses so rich that they could draw the gods down to the altars of China.

Immediately beyond the bronze pillars lay the long, narrow coastal nation of Champa and here, finally, was the limit of Hua expansion into the tropics. In post-Han times Champa was a great independent kingdom, ruled by a king clad in cotton, adorned with necklaces of gold and pearls and wearing flowers in his hair. He was protected by guards in rattan armour, who rode elephants into battle. Cham culture, like most cultures of South-East Asia, had been strongly modified by Indian institutions, including the religions of Shiva, Vishnu and the Buddha. The Chinese pushed continually at the borderland of the "malignant and tyrannical" Chams, while the Chams raided the Chinese settlements when they could.

Beyond Champa were the rich countries of the Gulf of Siam, the Java Sea and the Bay of Bengal. The conquests of Ma Yüan opened up sea routes to these enchanting emporia—but the glorious opportunities offered here to the Hua landlubbers could be only partially exploited. The dark waters of the South China Sea were a much greater barrier to the Chinese than the shifting sands of the Gobi Desert. Even as late as T'ang times, they continued to rely chiefly on foreign ships to transport them and their wares to the Indianized seaports of the fabulous south. Persian and Singhalese argosies, some 200 feet long and carrying more than 600 men, sailed from Canton on the winter monsoon that blew out of the north. They carried porcelain, musk and slaves along the coast of Champa, leaving rare gems, drugs and fine hardwoods for the Chinese aristocracy behind.

The few Chinese traders who braved these remote waters in foreign ships became accustomed to the black and malicious (as they thought) faces of the Indonesians. They brought back tales of the wild Nicobar where their vessels stopped for coconuts and ambergris on the way to Ceylon, the Island of Rubies; and they regaled listeners with accounts of depredations by pirates encountered on the way to the Indian coast and its rich stocks of saffron, sandalwood and ivory.

By medieval times, the ships from the Indian Ocean were pouring exotic items into Chinese cities. From Annam, now a part of both Vietnams, came silver to make ewers and vases; exotic dyes such as one called "dragon's blood", came from Indonesia; gamboge came from the resin of an Indo-Chinese forest tree. Fine tropical hardwoods were in great demand: dark sanderswood to make lutes and cabinet-work; red-brown rosewood for tables and couches; yellow Indian sandalwood for images, reliquaries and jewel boxes; ebony for the zithers of gentlemen. From the South Seas came all sorts of aromatic goods such as aloeswood, patchouli and cloves. The fortunate men of T'ang lived in a sparkling scented world, almost unparalleled in other places and times.

The treasure of trade goods was not the only lure to attract Chinese interest in distant lands. The most dedicated of the Chinese who took ship for the Indian Ocean were pious Buddhist pilgrims, many of them men of great attainments and universal culture. They went to the lands washed by the southern seas and there they found flourishing centres of Buddhism and other Indian religions.

The effects of the devoted energy and sufferings of migrant monks on Chinese civilization were immense. Driven by the prospect of religious merit to be gained by pilgrimages to the holy lands of India, and by the hope of obtaining the newest and purest products of religious scholarship in the form of reliable texts and the holiest relics, they plodded through the deserts of Central Asia, hacked their way through the jungles of Burma and risked the many dangers of the tropical seas. Their dedication was incredible. But they achieved great successes. The Buddhist monk I-ching left Canton in 671 to visit the sanctuaries and shrines of Indonesia and India. He returned in 695, after visiting 30 countries, with 400 collections of scriptures, the texts of 500,000 anthems and 300 holy relics.

The books of Buddhist South Asia had a tremendous influence on Chinese philosophy, science and ethics; they changed musical tastes; and the religious art of China was modified beyond recognition as a result of the study of the sacred paintings and statues of India and Greater Iran. The wandering monks also brought back Indian medical books, some of which were translated into Chinese; unfortunately, such translated works as "Brahman Medicinal Recipes" in five scrolls, and "Important Prescriptions Collected by Famous Physicians of the Western Regions" in four scrolls are now known only by title. More than books was brought back to China by devoted travellers. Their detailed accounts provided the first reliable information about distant countries whose terrain and customs had been known to the Chinese in only the sketchiest way. Probably the best of these pilgrim-explorers was Hsüan-tsang, who took the dangerous land route through Central Asia to India in the seventh century A.D. In later centuries he was immortalized as a saint and his journey popularized in fables and vernacular literature, but for the historian his great contribution was a wonderfully precise and colourful account of the many countries he traversed.

To take one example from among many, he describes Samarkand, today a provincial capital of the Uzbek region in Soviet Turkestan, but then a great imperial city, surrounded by a wall, about seven miles in circumference, which governed a powerful State. This was a rich land, he tells us, where the treasures of distant countries accumulated—full of powerful horses and skilled artisans, and blessed with a salubrious climate. He reports in measured four-word phrases:

Land, soil—fertile loam.
Sowing, reaping—fully planted.
Forest trees—dense, dark,
Flowers, fruit—prolific, thriving.

While the Chinese were taking their chances among strangers in strange lands, their foreign counterparts were bringing the flavours of their own cultures to China and getting a mixed reception. Royal personages and other dignitaries were likely to receive the best treatment, especially if they presented themselves as supplicants and friends. A particularly noble foreign refugee was Pērōz, son of the last king of Persia, who escaped to China when the Arabs overran his country in the seventh century; he was made an officer in the palace guard in Ch'ang-an.

Young Pērōz was seeking safety; others sought profit; still others learning. Japanese monks came regularly to Ch'ang-an to find learned instructors in the newest and most reliable interpretations of Buddhist scriptures, and the kings and noblemen of Tibet sent their sons to study the writings of Confucius and his followers.

The Chinese also gained from the influx of foreigners, many of them talented men who came to stay and who served their adopted land with distinction. In T'ang times, a proper education in the Chinese style could lead to success in the civil-service examinations, and to a respectable post in the administration. A Moslem who came to the capital in the middle of the ninth century excelled in the examinations and earned an important official post. A Sogdian merchant from Central Asia became Protector of Annam and that post was later held by a Japanese.

There were many establishments for the accommodation of foreigners, most of them founded by the alien communities themselves—hostels, wayside restaurants and temples—to make Korean envoys, Japanese monks, or Persian merchants more comfortable in this unfamiliar land. The alien communities took pains to show good will, often at considerable cost, towards their powerful hosts. The foreign community of Yang-chou at the mouth of the river Yangtze, for instance, which was composed of many nationalities, subscribed very substantial amounts of money towards the building of a government-sponsored Buddhist monastery in the ninth century.

In early T'ang times Persians were the most numerous and the most glamorous of the foreigners seen on the streets of Chinese cities. Their glamour derived from a popular belief that Persians were rich and that some were probably disguised noblemen. Perhaps some of the early Persian traders falsely passed themselves off as princely ambassadors to gain access to courtly circles. The richest trade in China was carried out under the name of "tribute", and who could tell what credentials foreign kings might provide? After the Arab conquest, many Persian aristocrats did, like the princely Pērōz, flee as far as China to seek refuge in the Chinese Court or to look for anonymous safety in the bustling T'ang markets.

After the middle of the T'ang period, when foreigners were rarer in the Middle Kingdom, the Persian became a common figure in popular tales. He was portrayed as being as rich as Croesus, a benefactor of young students, a wonder-worker, a connoisseur of gems and precious metals. He might be represented as avaricious and superstitious, but he was always elevated above common men because of his supposed princely birth and supernatural powers.

The average foreigner in China, however, was subject to severe disabilities, especially if he adhered to his native manners and customs. The dark-skinned, wavy-haired men of Cambodia and Malaya were called "ghosts", "goblins" and "demons" in some T'ang books. The orthodox Confucianists, though they were well enough educated to know that "foreign" and "non-human" were not synonymous, found all things foreign somewhat repellent—except, of course, for the rich tokens of submission to the Son of Heaven, which showed recognition of Chinese superiority. A rather chauvinistic poet of the ninth century deplored such regrettable manifestations as smelly woollen garments and odd-sounding music:

Ever since the foreign horsemen began raising
smut and dust,
Fur and fleece, rank and rancid, have filled
Ch'ang-an and Loyang.
Women make themselves foreign matrons, by
the study of foreign make-up;
Entertainers present foreign tunes, in their
devotion to foreign music.

But although the traditional moralists despised foreign ways and regretted their acceptance by honourable Hua men, they were not always able to prevail against the enticement of exotic goods and strange ideas. In fact, there was no area of Chinese life that was left untouched by alien ways.

Foreign nations contributed continuously to the ideas the Chinese had about the world, and enhanced the pleasure they took in it. India influenced Chinese astronomy and cosmology. The influence of the Sogdians, horse-breeders and caravaneers from the prosperous lands around Samarkand, can be traced in a list of the names of the sun, the moon and the major planets in a T'ang calendar. Venus appears there, for instance, as Nahid, an old Semitic Aphrodite. In some old-fashioned Chinese almanacs of our own time, the word for the "sun" in Sunday is still the Sogdian word "Mihr".

Popular tales and wonder stories came from India and Persia. Even the Greco-Roman world and its fringes made their contributions; the Chinese came to know the story of the pygmies and the cranes, which Homer knew; they had their own strange version of the Cinderella story; they could read of a witches' sabbath on a mountain-top very like the dark orgies featured in some Western tales. And in the wake of Buddhist philosophy came a host of moral parables.

With the decline, from Han times on, of the old symbolic art forms—the heritage of the Bronze Age—the art forms, the motifs and styles of Iran and the Hellenistic world infiltrated Chinese culture. Bunches of Greek-looking grapes ornament the backs of T'ang bronze mirrors, and the equestrian figures of Persian kings appear on the splendid many-coloured damasks of the same period. Devout T'ang Buddhists bowed before the painted forms of holy bodhisattvas, which were portrayed as languid Indian princes wearing strings of glittering jewels.

Foreign music could be heard at the Court, which, in early medieval times, maintained orchestras of native players and dancers from Cambodia, Burma and many States of Central Asia, all wearing their extraordinary native costumes. At the T'ang Court might be seen a Cambodian dance troupe wearing costumes of pink cotton and red leather shoes, and accompanied by a band of drums, flutes, pan-pipes, oboes, bronze cymbals and conch shells. Or there might be performances by the famous dancers from Kucha, clad in crimson and white trousers, their heads bound with red fillets; in this age, both the Cambodians and Kuchans were truly international entertainers, admired throughout the civilized East. Such wonders were not restricted to the imperial Court. In the streets of the major cities popular songs were sung to tunes once heard only far beyond the Gobi Desert or in the snowy mountains of Tibet.

Every aspect of T'ang daily life showed the evidence of the popular taste for exotic novelties. Some men of T'ang liked to sleep in sky-blue Turkish tents, in the very midst of the great capital, and many men and women wore the costumes of nomadic cavaliers. Imports from remote places lightened the lives of the aristocrats. They kept parrots from Indonesia, lap dogs from Samarkand and falcons from Korea. Fashion decreed that up-to-date matrons daub their foreheads with the golden orpiment of Cambodia and their cheeks with the crimson lac of Vietnam. Their tables boasted Tibetan kohlrabi, Manchurian mullet, Persian myrobalans, Korean pine nuts, and Indian pepper—to name only a few of the hundreds of marvellous delicacies available to the masters of the Eastern world.

The fact that the rich flavours of Asia had, after a thousand years, become commonplace in China was not unrelated to the profound belief that they rightly belonged there, for, in theory, the domain of the Son of Heaven had no boundaries. In reality Chinese culture had become increasingly receptive to the outer world. And the simpler, classical world of Szu-ma Niu, although it continued to be honoured in thought and writing, had vanished beyond the possibility of recovery.

ARISTOCRATS *like this well-dressed couple were frequent visitors at Court.*

ROYAL DAYS OF T'ANG

The T'ang Dynasty, which lasted from A.D. 618 to 907, was Ancient China's greatest period of enlightenment and prosperity, a time when the arts flourished and a brisk trade with the West drew many foreigners. The visitors brought with them strange foods, their own styles of clothing and new forms of entertainment, all of which influenced the emperor's Court in Ch'ang-an, China's bustling capital. Much of the spirit of those days has been preserved in ceramic figurines made by skilled T'ang artisans. Charming little statuettes representing courtiers and generals, musicians and acrobats, they were buried in the tombs of the well-to-do, serving as companions for the dead and reminders of the good life at Ch'ang-an.

Photographs by Leonard von Matt

A COURTLY LADY'S MODISH DRESS

Like women of every era, ladies of the T'ang Court were quick to adopt new fashions—the more exotic the better. The modish courtesan here, seen in three views, wears a costume and head-dress of distinctly eclectic taste. Her gown —with its tight bodice, deep neckline, wing-like shoulder projections and long, looped sleeves— was inspired by styles then popular in Central Asia. Her upswept hair-do and winged tiara echo Persian coiffures of the time.

Such stylish ladies figured importantly in Court life, and the annals of the day record that they were more frequently sought after for their beauty and intelligence than as concubines. Many of these courtesans became the insepar-able companions of the noblemen they served, and sometimes gained enormous political power.

THE WORK AND SPORT OF A GENERAL

During the T'ang era military victories enabled China to stretch its northern frontiers from the Sea of Japan to Central Asia. These conquests were led by hard-riding generals like the one depicted on the left. Wearing armour of tough rhinoceros hide, he and his fellow warriors took lands to the north and west of the Middle Kingdom and held them in the name of the emperor.

From time to time these powerful regional commanders were summoned to the emperor's Court to report on conditions in the provinces. While there they were entertained with magnificent feasts, and often a royal hunt in the Imperial Hunting Park. Such sport called for the skills of a falconer like the one seen in the figurine on the right, sitting lightly on his mount, his bird perched on his wrist, ready for the chase.

A PEDLAR OF EXOTIC WARES

Following the wars of consolidation in the seventh century, there was a period of peace in which trade flourished. Eager merchants came by land and sea to sell their goods, which included Persian rugs, ivory from Cambodia and

slaves from Java. The pedlar below, identified by his facial characteristics as a man of the Middle East, wears high boots with the trousers tucked in the top, a Persian mode of dress common throughout Asia. He carries his goods in a canopied, two-wheeled ox-cart. Many such traders risked the perils of overland travel to reach the capital's markets. Here, they haggled with buyers in a babel of tongues, lending to the city a competitive and cosmopolitan air.

NIMBLE PERFORMERS AT COURT

Visitors to the Court were treated to a variety of entertainment, which often included a wrestling match. Some of the wrestlers came from Central Asia, like the athlete below, who wears a soft cap and open tunic tied with a sash.

The antics of acrobats and tumblers were a constant source of delight to the Chinese people. Troupes like the one pictured above frequently toured the country, playing to paying audiences. The best of these were also invited to appear at the royal Court. Here they would regale the emperor and his guests with various tumbling stunts, including forward rolls and back-bends (bottom figures), trapeze acts (top left) and daring aerial somersaults.

SONGS FOR THE EMPEROR

Music and dancing were so loved by the T'ang Chinese that a special section of the royal palace in Ch'ang-an was set aside to help to train young students in these arts. It was called, simply, chiao-fang ("training centre") and

was attended by Indo-Chinese, Koreans and Indians, as well as Chinese girls. The most accomplished of its students played at Court, where no entertainment was complete without music and dancing by groups like this one. The four girls seated on the left sing, play mouth-organs of bamboo pipes and strum a lute. Their songs accompany three graceful dancers who, in the words of a Chinese poet, "turn, whirl and dance like the falling snow . . .".

CHRONOLOGY—*A listing of significant events in the history of Ancient China*

Date	Political and Military	Dynasty	Arts, Sciences and Religion
2000 B.C.	Era of the legendary Hsia Dynasty begins	HSIA DYNASTY	The potter's wheel is introduced Pigs, dogs, oxen, goats and sheep are domesticated The culture that was to leave the oldest archaeological evidence flourishes in China
1500 B.C.	The Shang Dynasty establishes and maintains a loosely organized authority over the settlements in the Yellow river valley Anyang, the Shang capital, is established, and imposing palaces, large irrigation works, warehouses and granaries are built	SHANG DYNASTY	A logographic system of writing, in which each written word is a stylized picture, is developed and first used by shamans on oracle bones to communicate with the spirit world Artisans master techniques of making beautiful bronze ritual vessels and stone and ivory carvings Armies use wheeled chariots and unique composite bows made of wood, reinforced by horn and sinew Water buffalo and several species of fowl are domesticated
1000 B.C.	Wu Wang, son of Wen Wang, semi-legendary king of the north-western State of Chou, conquers Shang and founds the dynasty of Chou An eclipse is recorded; later verified by modern astronomers, it was to give historians their first firm date in Chinese history Invasions force the weakened Chou rulers to move their capital eastwards from Ch'ang-an to Loyang Chou power declines with the rise of feudalism A written legal code is established Civil war begins in the Middle Kingdom, shattering Chou rule Cavalry tactics, armour and weapons are adopted from northern nomads Civil war between the city-States begins; they were to continue for almost two centuries, a time that was later known as the Period of the Warring States	CHOU DYNASTY	Some of the works later to be collected in the *Canon of Poetry* ("Book of Odes") and the *Book of History* are written Iron ploughs and swords come into wide use Confucius, sage and teacher, travels from one feudal Court to another preaching respect for tradition, morality and duty The semi-legendary Lao Tan preaches conformity with the Way of Nature, a system of belief later called Taoism Mo Tzu, an Anti-Confucianist, preaches love, non-aggression and utilitarianism Mencius, a follower of Confucius, teaches that man's nature is basically good Chuang Tzu, a mystic, writes poetic allegories about the interchangeability of life forms
221 B.C.	Rulers of the north-western State of Ch'in defeat other contenders and found the Ch'in Dynasty China becomes a centralized empire under Shih Huang Ti, the brutal First Emperor of Ch'in The Great Wall of China is built by linking together numerous ancient defensive walls along some 1,500 miles of China's northern border Shih Huang Ti's weak successor is murdered after a three-year reign The government establishes iron and salt monopolies China takes over control of North Korea	CH'IN DYNASTY	Customs duties, weights and measures and writing are standardized by Shih Huang Ti, the First Emperor of Ch'in Shih Huang Ti orders burning of books except religious, medical and agricultural texts
206 B.C.	Liu Pang leads a revolt against the Ch'in, founds the Han Dynasty and becomes known as Emperor Kao Tsu		Han Emperor institutes "Confucianism" as the State religion and orders the abolition of old nature worship Parts of the Confucian Classics are salvaged and rewritten

Li Shao-Chün, first known alchemist, claims to have found the secret of turning cinnabar into gold

HAN DYNASTY

0

Wang Mang usurps the Han throne and attempts many radical social reforms during his short interregnum

The revolt of the "Yellow Turbans", a Taoist cult, causes the final collapse of the official Han religion and contributes to the dynasty's collapse

Bore-holes 2,000 feet deep are drilled in the salt mines of Szechwan

Wang Ch'ung, brilliant and sceptical essayist, is born

Buddhist priests from India bring their doctrine to China

Paper is invented

Pan Ku writes his meticulous *History of the Former Han Dynasty*

Astronomical instruments are improved to make possible the accurate prediction of eclipses

Chang Heng, poet and astronomer, is the first to use water power to run an orrery, the ancestor of the modern clock

The Five Classics and the Analects are engraved in stone

Buddhism becomes a popular religion

Ko Hung, China's most famous alchemist, carries out experiments attempting to find the elixir of life

SIX KINGDOMS

A.D. 220

With the Han Dynastys' fall, nomads begin their invasions from the north: China is left without a stable government for almost four centuries

The Western Chin Dynasty tries to reunify China but abandons the north to the barbarians

The Sui Dynasty seizes power

Hsieh Ho lays down his famous Six Canons of Painting

Pictures related to the life of Buddha are painted on the walls of caves at Tun-Huang

The Empress Wu rebuilds the Luminous Palace

The supposed author of the *Lao Tzu* is canonized

T'ANG DYNASTY

A.D. 618

The T'ang Dynasty is founded by T'ai Tsung

Li Lung-chi (also known as Hsüan Tsung), greatest of the T'ang emperors, begins his long reign

An Lu-shan, an illiterate army officer, foments the rebellion that marks the decline of T'ang power

A Chinese Buddhist princess marries the first king of Tibet

Alien religions, including Buddhism, are intermittently proscribed

Li Tsu, last scion of the House of T'ang, is guest of honour at a banquet at which his nine brothers are murdered by the powerful war-lord Chu Ch'an-chung

Li Tsu abdicates, ending T'ang rule

Buddhist pilgrims, notably I-ching and Hsüan Tsang, penetrate western Asia

The Grand Canal is built, connecting Hangchow in the south with Ch'ang-an in the north

The poets Li Po, Tu Fu and Po Chü-i, and the famous polemicist Han Yü receive wide popular acclaim

Printing from woodblocks begins, and large printing presses are constructed

Gunpowder is invented and used in pyrotechnical displays

An astronomical clock is built at Ch'ang-an

Gautama Siddharta, an Indian astronomer working for the imperial observatory at Ch'ang-an, publishes his astrological almanac

Han Kan becomes famous for his paintings of the powerful Central Asian horses, called dragon-horses, that were being brought into the T'ang capitals

The new game of polo becomes popular among the T'ang *élite*

Chinese porcelain wins recognition for its excellence throughout Asia

The Diamond Sūtra is printed on government presses

A.D. 907

BIBLIOGRAPHY

The following volumes were selected during the preparation of this book for their interest and authority, and for their usefulness to readers seeking additional information on specific points. An asterisk (*) marks works available in both hard-cover and paperback editions; a dagger (†) indicates availability only in paperback.

TRANSLATIONS OF ANCIENT CHINESE WORKS

Chai, Ch'u and Winberg, *The Sacred Books of Confucius and Other Confucian Classics.* University Books, Bantam: Transworld, 1965.
Forks, Alfred, *Lun-Heng: Essays of Wang Ch'ung.* 2 vols. Paragon Book Gallery, New York, 1962.
Han-shan, *Cold Mountain.* Transl. by Burton Watson. Grove Press, Transworld, 1962
Legge, James, transl. *The I Ching** (The Book of Changes). Dover: Constable, 1963.
Legge, James, *The Chinese Classics,* vol. 1. Clarendon Press, 1893.
Pan Ku, *History of the Former Han Dynasty.* Waverly Press, 1944.
Steele, John, transl., *The I Li, or Book of Etiquette and Ceremonial.* Ch'eng-wen, Taipei, W. S. Hall, 1966.
Waley, Arthur:
The Analects of Confucius. George Allen & Unwin, 1938.
The Way and Its Power. Evergreen: Transatlantic, 1958.
Three Ways of Thought in Ancient China. Allen & Unwin, 1953.
Watson, Burton, *Records of the Grand Historian of China.* Translated from the *Shih Chi* of Szu-ma Chien. 2 vols. Columbia University Press, 1961.

GENERAL HISTORY

Bloodworth, Dennis, *The Chinese Looking-Glass.* Farrar, Straus, and Giroux: W. S. Hall, 1967.
Chang, Kwang-Chih, *The Archeology of Ancient China.* Yale University Press, 1963.
Chi, Li, *The Beginnings of Chinese Civilization.* University of Washington Press, 1957.
Creel, Herrlee Glessner, *The Birth of China.** Frederick Ungar, New York, 1964.
Eberhard, W. A., *A History of China.* University of California Press, Berkeley, 1950.
Fitzgerald, C.P.:
China: A Short Cultural History. Praeger: Transatlantic, 1961.
The Son of Heaven. Cambridge University Press, 1933.
Goodrich, L. C., *A Short History of the Chinese People.** Harper & Row, 1959.
Granet, Marcel, *Chinese Civilization.* * Meridian Book: Transatlantic, 1958.
Grousset, René, *The Civilizations of the East: China.* Knopf, W. S. Hall, 1934.
Hsu, Cho-yun, *Ancient China in Transition.* Stanford University Press, 1965.
Latourette, K. C., *The Chinese: Their History and Culture.* Collier-Macmillan, 1964.
MacNair, Harley Farnsworth, ed., *China* (The United Nations Series). University of California Press, 1951.
Maspero, Henri, *La Chine Antique.** Presses Universitaires de France: Zwemmer, 1965.
Pulleyblank, E. G., *The Background of the Rebellion of An Lu-Shan.* Oxford University Press, 1955.
Reischauer, Edwin O., and John K. Fairbank, *East Asia: The Great Tradition.* Houghton Mifflin: W. S. Hall, 1960.
Schulthess, Emil, *China.* The Viking Press: Transatlantic, 1966.
Soothill, W. E., *The Hall of Light.* Lutterworth Press, 1951.
Watson, William, *Early Civilization in China.* Thames and Hudson, 1966.

RELIGION AND PHILOSOPHY

Conze, Edward, ed., *Buddhist Texts through the Ages.* Philosophical Library: W. S. Hall, 1954.
Creele, H. G., *Confucius and the Chinese Way.* Harper & Row, 1960.
Ch'en, Kenneth K. S., *Buddhism in China: A Historical Survey.* Princeton University Press, 1964.
Dumoulin, Heinrich, *A History of Zen Buddhism.* Pantheon Books: W. S. Hall, 1963.
Eliade, Mircea, *Shamanism.* Bollingen Foundation, New York, 1964.
Fung Yu-Luan:
A History of Chinese Philosophy, 2 vols. Princeton University Press, 1952–3.
The Spirit of Chinese Philosophy. Transl. by E. R. Hughes. Kegan Paul, 1947.
Hughes, E. R., transl. and ed., *Chinese Philosophy in Classical Times.* J. M. Dent & Sons, 1942.
Fairbank, John K., ed., *Chinese Thought and Institutions.* University of Chicago Press, 1957.
Shyrock, John K., *The Origin and Development of the State Cult of Confucius.* Paragon Book Reprint Corp., New York, 1966.
Thomas, Edward J., *A History of Buddhist Thought.* Barnes and Noble: Transatlantic, 1933.
Thomas, Edward J., *The Life of Buddha as Legend and History.* Barnes and Noble: Transatlantic, 1952.
Waley, Arthur, *The Nine Songs: A Study of Shamanism in Ancient China.* Allen and Unwin, 1955.
Weber, Max, *The Religion of China.* The Free Press of Glencoe: Collier-Macmillan, 1951.
Wright, Arthur F., *Buddhism in Chinese History.* Stanford University Press, 1959.
Wright, Arthur F., ed., *Studies in Chinese Thought.* University of Chicago Press, 1953.

LITERATURE

Bishop, J. L., *Studies in Chinese Literature.** Harvard University Press, 1965.
Graham, A. C., *Poems of the Late T'ang.** Penguin Books, 1965.
Hightower, J. R., *Topics in Chinese Literature.** Harvard University Press, 1965.
Hughes, E. R., *Two Chinese Poets.* Princeton University Press, 1960.
Hung, William, *Tu Fu: China's Greatest Poet.** Harvard University Press, 1952.
Liu Wu-chi, *An Introduction to Chinese Literature.* Indiana University Press, 1966.
Rexroth, Kenneth, *One Hundred Poems from the Chinese.* † New Directions, New York, 1965.
Waley, Arthur:
The Poetry and Career of Li Po. Allen and Unwin, 1950.
Translations from the Chinese. Knopf: W. S. Hall, 1945.
Watson, Burton, *Early Chinese Literature.* Columbia University Press, 1962.

ARTS AND ARCHITECTURE

Boyd, Andrew, *Chinese Architecture.* University of Chicago Press, 1962.
Cahill, James, *Chinese Painting.* Editions d'Art Skira, New York, 1960.
Chang Chung-Yuan, *Creativity and Taoism: A Study of Chinese Philosophy, Art, and Poetry.* Julian Press: Edward Somerfield, 1963.
Ch'en Chih-mai, *Chinese Calligraphers & Their Art.* Melbourne University Press, Melbourne, 1966.
Fong, Wen, *Wang Hui and the Great Synthesis.* To be published in 1968 by Princeton University Press.
Grousset, René, *Chinese Art and Culture.* Orion: Transatlantic, 1959.
Jenyns, R. Soames, and William Watson, *Chinese Art: The Minor Arts,* 2 vols. Universe Books, 1963, 1965.
Lee, Sherman E., *A History of Far Eastern Art.* Harry N. Abrams, New York, 1964.
Lion-Goldschmidt, Daisy and Jean-Claude Moreau-Gobard, *Chinese Art.* Universe Books, 1962.
Loehr, Max, *Relics of Ancient China.* Asia House, New York, 1965.
Mai-Mai Sze, *The Tao of Painting.* Bollingen Foundation, New York, 1963.
Sachs, Curt:
The History of Musical Instruments. Norton: W. S. Hall, 1940.
The Rise of Music in the Ancient World. Norton: W. S. Hall, 1943.
Sickman, Lawrence, and Alexander Soper, *The Art and Architecture of China.* Penguin Books, 1960.
Swann, Peter C., *Chinese Monumental Art.* Viking Press: Transatlantic, 1963.
Watson, William, *Ancient Chinese Bronzes.* Faber & Faber, 1962.
Wellesz, Egon, *Ancient and Oriental Music.* Oxford University Press, 1957,
Willetts, William, *Foundations of Chinese Art.* Thames and Hudson, 1965.

SCIENCE AND TECHNOLOGY

Goodrich, C., *The Invention of Printing in China.* Ronald Press: Wheldon & Wesley, 1955.
Hume, Edward H., *The Chinese Way in Medicine.* Johns Hopkins Press, 1940.
Needham, Joseph, *Science and Civilization in China,* 4 vols. Cambridge University Press, 1962–1965.
Needham, J., Wang Ling, and D. J. Price, *Heavenly Clockwork.* Cambridge University Press, 1960.
Thorwald, Jürgen, *Science and Secrets of Early Medicine.* Harcourt, Brace and World, New York, 1963.
Tsien, T. H., *Written on Bamboo and Silk.* University of Chicago Press, 1962.
Wallnöfer, Heinrich, and Anna von Rottauscher, *Chinese Folk Medicine.* Crown Publishers: Heffer, 1965.

ECONOMICS, GEOGRAPHY AND DAILY LIFE

Ch'ao-Ting, Chi, *Key Economic Areas in Chinese History.* Allen and Unwin, 1936.
Cressey, George B., *Land of the 500 Million: A Geography of China.* McGraw-Hill, 1955.
Herrman, Albert, *A Historical Atlas of China.* Aldine: Bailey Bros., 1966.
Schafer, E. H., *The Golden Peaches of Samarkand.* University of California Press, 1963
Swann, Nancy Lee, *Food and Money in Ancient China.* Princeton University Press, 1950.
Tregear, T. R., *A Geography of China.* Aldine: Bailey Bros., 1965.
Twitchett, D. C., *Financial Administration under the T'ang Dynasty.* Cambridge University Press, 1963.
Van Gulik, R. H., *Sexual Life in Ancient China.* E. J. Brill, New York, 1961.

ACKNOWLEDGEMENT OF QUOTATIONS

Page 27: from *The Book of Songs,* trans. by Arthur Waley, Grove Press, 1960, p. 123. Pages 89, 95, 98: trans. courtesy British Museum. Page 123: Wang Wei, from *Introduction to Oriental Civilizations; Sources of Chinese Tradition,* compiled by Wm. Theodore de Bary, Wing-tsit Chan, Burton Watson, Columbia University Press, 1960, p. 295. Pages 151–152: Po Chü-i, from *Translations from the Chinese* by Arthur Waley, Alfred A. Knopf, 1941, pp. 157, 197. Page 154: Wang Wei, unpublished trans. by Burton Watson. Page 155: Han-shan, from *Cold Mountain,* trans. by Burton Watson, Grove Press, 1962, p. 66. Page 157: Kuo P'u, unpublished trans. by Burton Watson. Page 158: anonymous, unpublished trans. by Burton Watson. Page 159: Po Chü-i, from *Translations from the Chinese* by Arthur Waley, Alfred A. Knopf, 1941, p. 144. Pages 160–161: Tu Fu, from "Written Aboard a Boat", unpublished trans. by Burton Watson. Page 162: Szu-ma Hsiang-ju, from *Early Chinese Literature* by Burton Watson, Columbia University Press, 1962, p. 275.

ART INFORMATION AND PICTURE CREDITS

The sources for the illustrations in this book are set forth below. Descriptive notes on the works of art are included. Credits for pictures positioned from left to right are separated by semicolons, from top to bottom by dashes. Photographers' names that follow a descriptive note appear in parentheses. Abbreviations include "c." for century and "ca." for circa.

COVER—Civil official, ceramic tomb figurine, A.D. 618–906. Royal Ontario Museum (Leonard von Matt from Rapho Guillumette). 8–9—Map by Ed Young.

CHAPTER 1: 10—*Portrait of the Legendary Emperor Fu Hsi,* Ma Lin, colour and ink on silk, mid-13th c. A.D., National Palace Museum, Taipei (T. Tanuma); background courtesy Eikado East, New Hope, Pa. 13—*Ting,* bronze ritual vessel *ca.* 1500 B.C., courtesy Mr. and Mrs. F. Brodie Lodge, England (Derek Bayes). 16—Map by Rafael D. Palacios. 21–31—Bronze ritual and decorative objects, *ca.* 1500 B.C.–A.D. 220, Nelson Gallery of Art—Atkins Museum, Kansas City (Pete Turner).

CHAPTER 2: 32—Model of house, pottery, 206 B.C.–A.D. 221, Nelson Gallery of Art and Atkins Museum of Fine Arts, Nelson Fund, Kansas City (Ken Kay). 35—Warrior, ceramic tomb figurine, A.D. 525, Royal Ontario Museum, University of Toronto. 36–37—Maps by Rafael D. Palacios. 41—Men playing game called Liu Po, ceramic tomb figurines, 1st-2nd century A.D., courtesy of the Trustees of the British Museum (John R. Freeman) and *Early Civilization in China,* William Watson, Thames and Hudson, 43–55—Tomb tile rubbings, 200 B.C.–A.D. 200, Allen Memorial Art Museum, Oberlin College, Oberlin, Ohio (Lee Boltin).

CHAPTER 3: 56—Head, painted pottery, Neolithic, Museum of Far Eastern Antiquities, Stockholm (Dr. Heinz Zinram). 58—Dragon, bronze, 206 B.C.–A.D. 220, Smithsonian Institution, Freer Gallery of Art, Washington, D.C. 60—*Portrait of Confucius,* anonymous, paint on silk, National Palace Museum, Taipei. 62—Calligraphy by John Condon after original in *The Tao of Painting,* Mai-mai Sze, Pantheon Books, New York. 67—Buddhas, Mai-chi-shan, China, A.D. 386–1000 (Dominique Darbois). 68—Attendant figure, cave 60, Mai-chi-shan, China, *ca.* A.D. 535–556 (Claude Arthaud and François Hébert-Stevens). 69—Guardian figure, cave 43, Mai-chi-shan, China, extensively restored *ca.* A.D. 960–1127 (Claude Arthaud and François Hébert-Stevens). 70—The disciple, Kasyapa, cave 88, Mai-chi-shan, China A.D. 520–530 (Claude Arthaud and François Hébert-Stevens). 71—Head of a Lohan, Tun-huang, China, early 7th c. (Claude Arthaud and François Hébert-Stevens). 72–73—Seated bodhisattva, cave 15 A., Yün-Kang, China, *ca.* A.D. 486–496 (Claude Arthaud and François Hébert-Stevens). 74—Central Buddha, cave 20, Yün-Kang, China, 460–470 A.D. (Claude Arthaud and François Hébert-Stevens). 75—Head of Buddha, cave 102, Mai-chi-shan, China (Dominique Darbois); hands of Buddha, cave 127, Mai-chi-shan, China (Dominique Darbois); seated Buddha, Mai-chi-shan, China, A.D. 536–556 (Claude Arthaud and François Hébert-Stevens). 76–77—Buddha Vairocana flanked by bodhisattva and two guardians at Fang-hsien Temple, Lungmen, China, *ca.* A.D. 627–675 (Emil Schulthess from Black Star).

CHAPTER 4: 78—*Portrait of the Legendary Emperor Yu,* Ma Lin, *ca.* A.D. 1250, colour and ink on silk, National Palace Museum (T. Tanuma). 80—Jade pi, 1000–221 B.C., Museo Orientale Ceramiche, Hugues Le Gallais Collection, Venice (Emmett Bright). 84—Map by Rafael D. Palacios. 89–97—*Admonitions of the Instructress to the Court Ladies,* attributed to Ku K'ai-chih and variously designated a retouched original of A.D. 390–400 or a copy of A.D. 618–906, painted silk hand scroll, Benrido, Kyoto and Trustees of British Museum. 98–99—*Admonitions of the Instructress to the Court Ladies,* attributed to Ku K'ai-chih and variously designated a retouched original of A.D. 390–400 or a copy of A.D. 618–906 courtesy Trustees of the British Museum.

CHAPTER 5: 100—*The Filial Son,* sarcophagus, *ca.* A.D. 525, engraved limestone, Nelson Gallery of Art—Atkins Museum, Nelson Fund, Kansas City. 104—Tomb tile rubbing, 200 B.C.–A.D. 200. Allen Memorial Art Museum, Oberlin College, Oberlin, Ohio (Lee Boltin). 109—Map by Enid Kotschnig after original by Hiraoka Takeo. 111—Calligraphy by Chuang Yen. 112—*Animal Fight in Shang-Lin Park,* anonymous, *ca.* 2nd–4th c. A.D., Ross Collection, Museum of Fine Arts, Boston (Frank Lerner). 113—Calligraphy by Chuang Yen; detail of photo page 112; calligraphy attributed to Wang Hsi-chih, 8th c. A.D., Japanese Imperial Household (Asahi Shimbun Publishers). 114—Calligraphy by Chuang Yen; "Palace Concert" (and detail from same painting) anonymous, 10th c. copy of 9th c. original, National Palace Museum, Taipei (T. Tanuma). 116—Calligraphy by Chuang Yen; "Mandala of Kuan-yin", anonymous, painting on silk from Cave of Thousand Buddhas, China, *ca.* A.D. 900, Musée Guimet (Agraci). 117—"Temptation and Assault by Mara", anonymous, painting on silk from Cave of Thousand Buddhas, China, *ca.* A.D. 900, Musée Guimet (Agraci). 118—Top two drawings from *Mustard Seed Garden Manual of Painting,* 17th c., as reproduced in *The Tao of Painting,* Mai-mai Sze, Pantheon Books, New York; bottom two illustrations from *Clearing after Snowfall,* 15th c. copy of 8th c. scroll by Wang Wei, ink on silk, Ogawa Collection, Kyoto (T. Tanuma). 119—Calligraphy by Chuang Yen; drawing from *Mustard Seed Garden Manual of Painting,* 17th c. as reproduced in *The Tao of Painting,* Pantheon Books, New York, *Clearing after Snowfall,* 15th c. copy of 8th c. scroll by Wang Wei, ink on silk, Ogawa Collection, Kyoto (T. Tanuma). 120—Calligraphy by Chuang Yen; *Clearing after Snowfall,* left detail from Ogawa Collection copy of *Clearing after Snowfall* scroll and right detail from Honolulu Academy of Arts Collection copy of *Clearing after Snowfall* (Raymond Sato). *Clearing after Snowfall* 16th c. copy of 8th c. scroll by Wang Wei, colour on silk, Honolulu Academy of Arts Collection, Honolulu (Raymond Sato). 121—*Clearing after Snowfall,* 15th c. copy of 8th c. scroll by Wang Wei, ink on silk, Ogawa Collection, Kyoto (T. Tanuma). 122—Calligraphy by Chuang Yen; *The Emperor's Horse "Shining Light of Night",* attributed to Han Kan, ink on silk, probably 8th c., Sir Percival and Lady David Collection, London (John R. Freeman). 123—*Scholar Fu Sheng,* attributed to Wang Wei, 8th c., ink on silk, Osaka Municipal Museum, Osaka (T. Tanuma).

CHAPTER 6: 124—The Tun-huang manuscript star-map, *ca.* A.D. 940, Trustees British Museum (Derek Bayes). 129—*Village Doctor at Work,* Li T'ang, colour on silk, 12th c., National Palace Museum, Taipei (T. Tanuma). 133–139—Drawings by Ed Young.

CHAPTER 7: 140—*Scholars Collating Classic Texts,* anonymous, colour on silk, 11th c., Museum of Fine Arts, Ross Collection, Boston. 142—Calligraphy by John Condon after original in *Foundations of Chinese Art,* William Willetts, Thames and Hudson, London. 144–145—Ch'u manuscript, silk, *ca.* 600 B.C., Sackler Collections, New York. 151—Photograph by Emil Schulthess from Black Star. 152–153—Photograph by Hélène Hoppenot. 154–155—Photograph by Emil Schulthess from Black Star. 156–157—Photograph by Dmitri Kessel. 159—Photograph by Marc Riboud from Magnum; photograph by Takayuki Senzaki. 160–161—Photograph by Paolo Koch from Black Star. 162–163—Photograph by Emil Schulthess from Black Star.

CHAPTER 8: 164—*Portrait of the Emperor Tau T'sung,* anonymous, 14th–17th copy of 7th–10th c. original, National Palace Museum, Taipei (T. Tanuma) background courtesy Eikado East, New Hope, Pa. 166–167—*Wen-chi's Captivity in Mongolia and Return to China,* detail, anonymous, ink on silk, 12th Century, Museum of Fine Arts, Ross Collection, Boston (Frank Lerner). 168–169—Map by Rafael D. Palacios. 173–183—Glazed pottery tomb figurines, *ca.* 200 B.C.–A.D. 900, Royal Ontario Museum, University of Toronto (Leonard von Matt from Rapho Guillumette).

ACKNOWLEDGEMENTS

For help given in the preparation of this book, the editors are particularly indebted to Gari K. Ledyard, Assistant Professor, Department of East Asian Languages and Culture, Columbia University, and Alexander Soper, Professor, Art Institute, New York University. The editors are also indebted to Wen C. Fong, Professor, Department of Art and Archeology, Princeton University; Laurence Sickman, Director and Curator of Oriental Art, Nelson-Atkins Gallery, Kansas City, Missouri; Peter C. Swann, Director, and Barbara Stephen, Assistant Curator, Far Eastern Department, Royal Ontario Museum; Burton Watson, Associate Professor of Chinese, and L. Carrington Goodrich, Dean Lung Professor Emeritus of Chinese, Columbia University; Jan Fontein, Curator, Department of Asiatic Art, Boston Museum of Fine Arts; Richard C. Rudolph, Professor of Oriental Languages, Department of Oriental Languages, University of California, Los Angeles; Jean Gordon Lee, Curator, Oriental Department, Philadelphia Museum of Art; Philip Mazzola, Sackler Collections, New York; Francis J. Caro, New York City; George Yeh, Minister without Portfolio, Executive Yuan, Republic of China, Taipei; James Wei, Director, Government Information Office, Republic of China, Taipei; Chiang Fu-Chung, Director, Chuang Yen, Deputy Director, Na Chih-Liang, Department Chief, and Li Lin-Tsan, Curator, National Palace Museum, Taipei; Ignatius Pao Tsun-Peng, Director, Ho Hao-Tien, Department Chief, and Chin Chi-Ti, Secretary, National Museum of History, Taipei; Wang Shih-Chien, President and Hsu Cho-Yun, Academia Sinica, Taipei; Chuang Pen-Li, Executive Director, Chinese Classical Music Association, Taipei; John M. Warner, Director, City Hall Museum and Art Gallery, Hong Kong; Imperial Household, Tokyo; Kikutaro Saito, Tokyo; Alice Boney, Tokyo; Seiichi Mizuno and Professor Hiraoka Takeo, Institute for the Humanistic Sciences, and Shigeyasu Hasumi, Aesthetic Section, Faculty of Letters, Kyoto University; Hiromi Ogawa, Kyoto; Y. Ernest Satow, Kyoto; Hiroshi Doi, Director, Executive Offices, Shosoin, Nara; Ryuichi Imamura, Director, and Masahiko Sato, Chief of Cultural Section, Municipal Art Museum, Osaka; Claude Arthaud Stevens, François Hébert-Stevens, Hélène Hoppenot, Paris.

INDEX

★ This symbol in front of a page number indicates an illustration of the subject mentioned.

Z

Typesetting by Alfred Utesch, Hamburg
Smeets Lithographers, Weert, Printed in Holland
Bound by Proost and Brandt N. V., Amsterdam